THE
SWORD-DANCES
OF
NORTHERN ENGLAND

THE
SWORD-DANCES
OF
NORTHERN ENGLAND

CECIL J. SHARP.

EP Publishing Limited
1977

Originally published in three parts
by Novello & Co, Ltd, London

Republished 1977 by
EP Publishing Limited
East Ardsley, Wakefield
West Yorkshire, England

Copyright © 1977 EP Publishing Limited

Reprinted 1978

ISBN 0 7158 1211 4

Please address all enquiries to EP Publishing Limited
(address as above)

Printed in Great Britain by
The Scolar Press Limited
Ilkley, West Yorkshire

The Sword Dancers

(From a Photo, by the People Studio.)

EARSDON SWORD-DANCE.

THE DANCERS HAVE JUST TIED THE NUT AND ARE "STEPPING" *(see p. 83).*

THE
SWORD DANCES

OF

NORTHERN ENGLAND

TOGETHER WITH

THE HORN DANCE

OF

ABBOTS BROMLEY

COLLECTED AND DESCRIBED

BY

CECIL J. SHARP.

TO

C. Lennox Gilmour.

PREFACE.

THE Author wishes to acknowledge the kindness and friendly help he has received from the dancers whose performances are described in this book, especially from Mr. T. Armstrong, the veteran Captain of the Earsdon team, and Messrs. Spence, Wragg and Harrison, the leaders respectively of the Earsdon, Grenoside, and Kirkby Malzeard dancers. He is also deeply indebted to Mrs. Eden, the Rev. Reginald and Mrs. Gatty, Dr. Michael Foster, Mr. J. E. Taylor, Mr. Parker Brewis, and Mr. W. Mill, and many others whose names are too numerous to mention, for the valuable and generous assistance they have, in one way or another, given him in the course of his investigations.

To Mr. E. Phillips Barker the Author owes a large debt of gratitude, not only for reading the proofs and bringing a wide, practical knowledge to bear upon his criticisms of the technical portions of the book, but also for materially helping him in the writing of the Introduction, of which he is to be regarded as joint-author.

Finally, he wishes to thank Mr. Ralph Hedley and the proprietors of the *Newcastle Weekly Chronicle* for permission to reproduce the former's picture in the frontis-piece; to Mr. W. Mill and Mr. A. Parker for allowing him to print the photographs facing p. 46 and p. 105; and to Messrs. James Bacon and Sons (Leeds and Newcastle) for permission to reproduce the photograph facing p. 51.

CONTENTS.

CHAPTER II.

CHAPTER III.

INTRODUCTION.

OF the four sword-dances described in these pages, two were collected in Yorkshire, one in Durham, and one in Northumberland. The long-sword Yorkshire dances differ very considerably from those gathered in the more northern counties, where the short-sword or "rapper" is used. The particular dances selected for publication are, I believe, typical examples of the two species of sword-dance.

The Abbots Bromley Horn-Dance is included for several reasons. Firstly, its movements, though few and very simple, possess a peculiar and characteristic beauty which makes it worthy of publication. Secondly, though the horn-dance is well known by repute to most antiquaries, and has often formed the subject of remark and discussion in archæological works, its figures have not yet, so far as I am aware, been technically described. Finally, the horn-dance and sword-dance, as I shall presently show, belong so far to the same order of ideas, that their juxtaposition is by no means inappropriate.

The purpose of this book is primarily practical. Its design is to place before those who are interested in the revival of our national dances some examples of a particular type of folk-dance which has not hitherto attracted the attention of collectors, and to present these in such a form that they may be learned without the aid of a special instructor and by those who have never seen the dances performed. Whether this object has been attained must be left to the decision of those to whom the book is addressed. It can however be said in all sincerity, that no trouble has been spared to note the dances with all possible accuracy, and to find simple and unambiguous language in which to describe them.

The sword-dance, like the Morris, is traditionally a man's dance. It is essentially an indoor dance, and can be performed in a room of ordinary size; its movements are vigorous, and the figures so varied and intricate that the performance makes equal demands on both mind and body.

To the folk-lorist the dances will make a different appeal. The sword-dance very obviously bears upon it the stamp of a high antiquity: its roots, stretching far into an unhistoried past, take hold upon the primal needs and rudimentary beliefs of primitive man. The whole folk-dance, indeed, is a riddle of which the answer, if we could but read it, would materially add to existing knowledge of the religious ideas and ceremonies, the dim faiths, fears and aspirations of our remotest ancestors. Doubtless the sword-dance is now and has been for innumerable generations practised for its intrinsic æsthetic and social qualities, and primarily for the sake of mere entertainment; yet originally there was in it another and deeper purpose. To discover that purpose is to solve a problem of great complexity. In an attempt to recover the significance of customs whose beginnings lie wrapped in the haze of prehistoric times, and whose inner meaning has been lost perhaps for ages before the observer's eye was turned on them, there is a wide field for difference of opinion, for different marshalling and interpretation of too scanty facts which must so often be eked out by more or less precarious conjecture. For the solution now to be offered, the writer does not claim that it is either final or original: he has only endeavoured to give, conformably to the scope and intention of this book, a coherent expression to a view which in his opinion agrees with the evidence previously acquired, and especially with the new evidence available in the dances now for the first time published in a detailed form.

What is a Morris-dancer? Anyone who is familiar with the normal Morris-dance of the Midlands and the South of England will be ready with an answer. But let him question the sword-dancers of Grenoside and Earsdon, and he will find them also insisting that they are Morris-dancers. Next let him follow up a few vague, verbal clues of supposed Morris-dancers, in the hope of discovering the Morris-dance proper: he will find time after time that he has been sent in quest of mummers—a class to him quite distinct. In due course it will dawn on him that the sword-dancer of Northern England, the Morris-dancer of the Midlands and the South, and the mummer of all England and Scotland, are in the pópular view as one, and pass under the same name. This is at least a significant point: a common name suggests other points of community—perhaps community of origin. Let us see whether further evidence will justify the ascription of a common source to these three forms of folk-entertainment.

The sword very naturally suggests itself as a starting-point. It is obviously the very life and soul of the sword-dance. In the mumming drama we find it playing an invariable and essential part which must be reserved for later notice. For the present we will concentrate our attention upon the Morris-dance proper, with which its connection is at first by no means so evident.

To this day the procession of Morris-dancers at Bampton (Oxfordshire) is headed by a man who carries a sword impaling a cake decorated with flowers and ribbons. The same custom was observed at Ducklington, Field Assarts and Leafield (Oxfordshire), Sherborne (Gloucestershire), and probably at many other places as well. Again, at Ruardean, Mayhill, Cliffords Mesne, and other villages in and around the Forest of Dean, the leader of the Morris-procession carried two swords, one in each hand, which he manipulated in a very skilful manner.

In Johnson's Dictionary (1755) the Morris is defined as "a dance in which bells are jingled or staves *or swords* clashed"; and Miss Burne in *Shropshire Folk-Lore* (p. 478), records that "some call the staves wooden swords," and prints a document (1652) in which mention is made of a "morrice-daunce . . . . with six sword bearers," one of whom,

Thomas Lee, " was most abusive." In two passing notices we seem to catch a hint of the transition from sword to stick in the dance itself. Bell (*Ballads and Songs of the Peasantry of England*), in his note on a Durham sword-dancers' song and interlude, says that the Devonshire peasants had a similar performance, with laths for swords.   Wright (*Dialect Dictionary, s.v.* Morris) records a Northamptonshire stick-dance, called the "Bedlam Morris," containing a figure which is otherwise only known in sword-dances.   More direct evidence may be cited.   At Flamborough (Yorks), where the sword-dance is still performed, the dancers use stout wooden swords, made of ash ; and in Sussex, Miss Lucy Broadwood tells me, the mummers, without actually dancing, still preserve traces of the circular sword-dance movement, and carry wooden swords which they lock together in the usual way.

With these indications of the sword's mere presence we must, so far as tradition and observed custom go, rest content. And so far indeed, it might be urged that in the sword-dance and Morris-dance the sword was merely a theatrical property, a convenient instrument for the purpose of the dance, like the broom in the broom-stick dance and the flail in the flail-dance, choice naturally falling on the sword in days when many wore and more possessed that weapon.   Yet it is hard to think that even so it would be the obvious implement of the dancing peasant ?   An examination of the possible significance of the sword in its relation to the Morris may carry us further.

For the Morris-dance of Mid-England, Mr. Percy Manning (*Folk-Lore*, viii. (1897), pp. 307-324) has gathered some most important facts.

He has shown that within living memory it was the custom in certain Oxfordshire villages to kill an animal for the purpose of a feast, at Whitsuntide and other Morris festivals. At Kirtlington, for instance, on the Monday, Tuesday and Wednesday after Trinity Sunday, a man walked before the

Morris-dancers carrying on his shoulders a lamb decked with ribbons and with its legs bound together. On the Wednesday it was killed and made into pies, one of which—the "head-pie"—contained the animal's head with wool intact. These pies were afterwards cut up and distributed, special virtue attaching to the head-pie, which could only be bought whole for a shilling. At Kidlington a similar "Lamb Ale," with some differences of detail, took place on Whit-Monday : a feast on the flesh of the lamb closed the proceedings.

Another custom formerly prevailing among certain villages on the western border of Oxfordshire, near what was once the great Forest of Wychwood, was the "Whit Hunt." These villages joined in hunting and killing three deer. The deer were skinned, the heads and antlers going to the three men who were first in at the death, while pieces of the skin were distributed as bringing luck. During the Hunt we learn that at Ducklington (selected by Mr. Manning as typical of the group), at Bampton (where this part of the custom still survives), and presumably in the other villages concerned, Morris-dancers went through the village, a man walking at their head with the large cake impaled on a sword to which reference has been made.

Indications of a similar custom might have been seen, as recently as seven to ten years ago, at Abingdon (Berkshire), where the Morris-dancers were preceded by (1) a man bearing a pair of ox's horns mounted on a pole ; (2) the "Mayor," carrying a money-box attached to a scarf round his neck, and a sword, or rather fencing foil, wrapped in white rag and decked, point and hilt, with white ribbons ; (3) the "ex-Mayor," holding a wooden cup or chalice, called "the glass," ornamented with a bull's heart in silver.

Now an outstanding feature in the religion of primitive communities is the periodic slaughter of some animal to provide a clan-feast. This was not at all a mere merry-making : it was a solemn sacrament. The primitive mind drew no very clear line between its dimly conceived clan-deity, the human members of the clan, and the sacred animals of the clan herd. There was close kinship between gods and men, men and animals, animals and gods. The clan, regarded as a common mass of flesh and blood, the clan god and the sacred animal strangely linked with his life, were of one kindred. To cement the bond between the members of the clan, and between the god and the clan, the most obvious means was that god and men together should be sharers in a ceremonial feast, together drinking the blood and eating the flesh of an animal victim in some mystic way identified with the god himself, the communion thus established, in the distribution of a divine life immanent in flesh and blood, conferring benefits on all the human participants.

It was not till a later stage of religious development that the victim so sacrificed was conceived as an oblation : godhead had grown less brotherly and more majestic, to be propitiated with gifts like the great ones of the earth; no longer as mystic eater and eaten to be present at our table and form our food.

Now may we not still see in the lamb-pies of Kirtlington, in the "lamb-ale" of Kidlington with its feast on the flesh of the slaughtered lamb, and in the final banquet of venison in the Whit Hunt, the last vestiges of the older sacramental sacrifice ? And may we not see the same in an Easter Monday ceremony at Hallaton,* in Leicestershire, where a hare (always a highly mysterious animal) is carried in procession, and "hare pies" afterwards scrambled for ? Though of course the meaning of the rite, in all these cases, has long been extinct except in a vague feeling that the participation in the meal, or the possession of a pie, "brings luck."

But a further primitive means of sacramental union with the deity lay in the worshipper's assuming the form of the slaughtered victim by robing himself in its head and skin.

* E. K. Chambers : *The Mediæval Stage*, i. 150.

Thus fortified inwardly with divine food and outwardly wearing the likeness of the divine, he would express his exaltation by appropriate movements, steps and gestures.

A survival of this metamorphosis is to be seen in the carrying of the horns by the six dancers at Abbots Bromley, and in the distribution of the heads and pieces of the skin of the slain deer at the Whit Hunt.

From the earliest times the head, as the special seat of the soul, was a thing of power, too dynamic, in fact, to be eaten, but a desirable if rather awful possession. So when circumstances forbade that a worshipper should receive the whole skin, and division was resorted to, the head was the part most prized, and became a reward of prowess, or later, when its awfulness had diminished, an object of sometimes fierce competition. The men who were first in at the death received the antlered heads in the Wychwood Forest custom. At Kirtlington the " head pie " (hardly intended to be eaten, one imagines) was only sold for a shilling. In ancient Rome two of the City wards met annually in a scrimmage for the head of the October Horse, and without adducing the detailed evidence, it may be stated that the games of football which are or were held yearly at certain places—as Alnwick, Chester and Dorking—are probably traceable to the same origin. The significance of the rabbit's head and skin on the Grenoside Captain's helmet may be discussed later.

At Ducklington and Bampton, two of the villages participating in the Whit Hunt, and presumably typical of the group, we saw that a sword and cake were carried before the Morris-dancers left behind in the village during the Hunt. No victim is recorded. At the Kirtlington and Kidlington Morris-festivals a lamb (at Kidlington its skin) was carried, but sword and cake are absent. Other resemblances in the customs are so many and so close that their original identity can hardly be questioned. Sword and lamb were instrument and victim—both sacrificial : in one district the sword has apparently vanished, in the other the lamb. A conjecture—

but it is only conjecture—may perhaps supply the reason. The proximity of Wychwood Forest may in the one case have occasioned the rise of a district hunters' rite alongside of the local agricultural rites of the various villages. For some reason the hunters' victim ousted the others, but the sword, as ensign of the village ceremony, was the more jealously preserved. Kidlington and Kirtlington, away to the East, and more purely agricultural, continued to slay their own victims, without the same spur to their conservatism in the choice of an instrument.

The meaning of the cake is dubious: it may be a substitute for an animal victim: on the other hand it may belong to a cognate rite. The sacrificial cake, made in a special manner of various kinds of grain, and eaten sacramentally, or carried away piece-meal and buried in the fields, is a well attested phenomenon of primitive religion.

As the sacrificial cake supplies a vegetable parallel to the animal victim, so the wearing of the victim's skin is paralleled by the wearing of a frame covered with green leaves and flowers, exemplified by Jack-in-the-Green in many May-Day ceremonies, and by the bearer of the Garland at Castleton in Derbyshire.

So far we have shown by scraps of tradition, and the evidence of customs either now surviving or observed not so long ago, that the sword had and still has a certain connection with the Morris-dance. The connection has dwindled, but its tenacity at least is proved by the centuries that have elapsed since the Morris-dance lost its definite religious significance, and became a mere form of healthy amusement, and social entertainment. If the theory of origin above applied to the midland Morris-festival be accepted, it assigns to the sword an organic status as the trace of a very primitive form of sacrifice. Our whole position will be greatly strengthened if we find in the other two branches of folk-custom, in which the sword still plays a more essential part—the sword-dance and the mumming play—any features which point to an origin related to or identical with that assumed in the case of the Morris-dance.

To the first of these we will now turn. And here we are able to supplement the descriptions contained in this volume with written records of the dance as it was performed in former centuries, and in this and other countries. This is in marked contrast to the past history of the Morris-dance, of which we know only a few meagre details of the characters who took part in the dance, their costume, and the bare fact of its distribution over Germany, Flanders, Switzerland, Italy, Spain and France. So far as I am aware, not a single detailed and technical description of the dance itself, as it was performed in days gone by, has come down to us, so that the whole of the technical knowledge we possess is confined to the dance as it appears in present or recent times.

Happily this is not so with the sword-dance. We know that it has been found all over Germany, in Sweden, in the Hebrides, in Fifeshire; in Spain, France, and the north of England, while traces have been observed in two of the southern English counties. The dance known in Italy as the *mattacino*, in Spain as the *matachin*, and in France as the *danse des bouffons*, in which apparently sword *and buckler* were used, is a form probably contaminated by the spectacular armed dances of Greek and Roman civilization, which were very far from being folk-dances in their later developments.

But in addition to this, records of the dance have survived which contain a certain amount of detailed description. The most systematic collection of these is K. Müllenhoff's monograph *Ueber den Schwerttanz* (*Festgaben für G. Homeyer :* Berlin, 1871, pp. 111-147). From this and some other sources the following summary has been drawn.

Leaving out of account the often quoted description given by Tacitus (*Germania*, 24), which is too cursory to be of much value, the earliest contemporary record known refers to a sword-dance at Brunswick, *c.* 1443.

But at Nuremberg tradition states that the cutlers performed their sword-dance in the year 1350 or 1351, and records of its repeated performance between the years 1490 and 1600 are or were in existence.

There is to be seen at Berlin a most instructive picture of the dance as it was performed at Nuremberg on February 23rd in the latter year. It shows two double rings of dancers in white shirts or doublets, holding up on a frame of interlaced swords two swordsmen clad entirely in colours. There are also, separately, seven sword-dancers, six in white doublets, the first only clothed in red, like one of the swordsmen. They dance in file toward the left, each sloping his own sword back over his left shoulder and grasping the sword-point of the man next in front of him. The last man only shoulders his sword. Pipe and tabour supply the music.

At Ulm in 1551 a sword-dance was performed by four-and-twenty journeymen, with two "masters of the long-sword." As the climax, all danced round a Fool, on whose shoulders each laid his sword; when the swords lay thus one of the masters of fence mounted on them. It is hard to see how he did it!

Olaus Magnus* is the first author to give a connected description of the dance, as practised among the Goths and Swedes, with some detail. "For eight successive days," he writes, "before Shrovetide, young men disport themselves in a rhythmic dancing measure, moving with swords held aloft but sheathed in a thrice-repeated round. Next they unsheath their swords, lift them once more, and extend them from hand to hand: circling more sedately, the swords grasped hilt and point between them, they change their order and bring themselves into position for forming a hexagonal figure which they call the Rose: this they undo forthwith by drawing back their swords and raising them, so that a square rose is formed over each man's head: finally they end their

---

* *De Gentibus Septentrionalibus* (Romæ, 1555) l. xv. c.xxiii.

display by a reverse movement, dancing very rapidly and clashing the flat of their swords together with the greatest vigour. The time of the performance is marked by pipe or singing or both together : the dance is at first staid, then grows faster and faster till it ends at a furious speed."

Johann Justus Winkelmann, writing in 1697, gives some particulars of the sword-dance in Hesse and Hersfeld. The dancers wore white shirts, hats decorated with coloured ribbons and white kerchiefs, sashes round the waist and bells at the knee : their sleeves were bound with ribbons which hung in long streamers. Their numbers were sixteen to twenty, and they performed at Shrovetide and at weddings. The leader speaks a rhymed prologue of a suspiciously archæological tinge, and after the dance, which is dismissed with a few words on its complexity, a rhymed epilogue of a more popular character and containing traces of impersonation. One phrase in it may perhaps justify the conjecture that he was hoisted meanwhile, presumably on a frame of swords.

The sword-dance in Ditmarschen is mentioned, and only mentioned, by Neocorus (*c.* 1600) : the jurist Anton Viethen (18th century) gives a detailed notice of it.

Viethen says that the dancers wore white shirts decked all over with gay ribbons, and one bell on each leg. All are bareheaded except the leader, whom they call "king," and an anonymous personage "in the middle" (*der so in der mitten*) whose part in the proceedings is not explained, but might correspond to that of the Fool. After a speech by the "king," the tabour strikes up and the dance begins. They dance in a ring; then hey (*tanzen kreuzweis durcheinander*); they jump over the swords ; they lay them down in a figure "not unlike a rose"; round this they dance in a ring and jump over it ; a square rose is formed on each dancer's head : finally they lock their swords, upon which the "king" steps and is hoisted and held while he says a few words of thanks to the onlookers. The number of dancers is not given.

An account of a sword-dance called the Bacchu-Ber*, performed at Cervières, is given in a book on the district of the Hautes Alpes, published at Paris in 1820. The dancers are nine, eleven or thirteen in number; the swords are broad, short and pointless. A special tune is used.

The dancers form a circle hilt-and-point: they lay down their swords radiating outwards from the centre; each salutes toward the right, beginning with the leader: then the swords are picked up, the hilt-and-point circle formed again, and they dance round. They make movements which bring each dancer's right wrist beneath his left elbow and his left wrist in front of his hip, " execute a *pas de deux* towards the left," and so return to the hilt-and-point circle. After this, led by the leader's left-hand neighbour, all pass, without loosing, under the leader's sword: at the end the leader turns round and takes up the same position as the rest. Next " all make a movement of the heels, at the same time raising the left hand above the head so as to place their neighbour's weapon on their right shoulder "—apparently an inversion of the usual hilt-and-point shouldering movement.

Then " the choragus (leader) after returning to his previous position, moves into the centre, and always continuing to hold the hilt and point of the two swords, he raises both hands to the level of his head; the others all crowd round him, doing the same with their weapons. The choragus then puts the two swords he holds on each shoulder; the others place theirs upon them, so that all the swords are crossed round his neck in a horizontal position. The dancers, when thus all grouped round the choragus, make several turns or movements to the left and jump about in time to the music. The choragus then brings his two swords down in front of him, and stands with his arms crossed, holding always the point of the one and the hilt of the other weapon; the rest follow his example and return to their positions."

* Translated by Mrs. J. C. Murray Aynsley, *Folk Lore Journal* v. (1887), pp. 312-314.

A figure follows in which the dancers break-up, apparently, into groups, various frames and triangles being formed with the swords. Finally all return to position and end with " a Pyrrhic salute "—whatever that may be.

Of the English accounts by far the most precise and most important is that given by Sir Walter Scott in a note to " The Pirate." Scott derived it from a copy of " a very old manuscript " made by William Henderson of Papa Stour, one of the Shetland Islands. Hibbert, in his *Description of the Shetland Islands* (Edinburgh, 1822), published a version of the same manuscript with alterations and interpolations.

The performance begins with a long prologue recited by the Master in the character of St. George, in which the dancers are described and introduced as in the Kirkby and Earsdon dances. Including the Master, the dancers are seven, bearing the names of the Seven Champions of Christendom.

The account of the dance itself is so interesting that it merits transcription in full. Scott's text is given, with Hibbert's variations, which are not without their value, in square brackets.

" The six stand in rank with their swords reclining on their shoulders. The Master (St. George) dances, and then strikes the sword of James of Spain, who follows George, then dances, strikes the sword of Dennis, who follows behind James. In like manner the rest—the music playing—swords as before. After the six are brought out of rank. they and the master form a circle and hold the swords point and hilt. [The Champions then extend their swords out at full length, when each of them is seen to grasp his own sword with his right hand, and the point of his neighbour's sword with his left hand; and being thus formed into a circle, hilt and point, as it is named—] This circle is danced round twice. The whole, headed by the master, pass under the swords held in a vaulted manner. They jump over the swords. This naturally places the swords across, which they disentangle by passing under their right sword [—each dancer passing under his right-hand sword]. They take up the seven swords, and form a circle, in which they dance round. [A single roundel, hilt and point, is then performed as before.]

"The master runs under the sword opposite, which he jumps over backwards. The others do the same. He then passes under the right-hand sword, which the others follow, in which position they dance, until commanded by the master, when they form into a circle and dance round [swords tended and grasping hilt and point] as before. They then jump over the right-hand sword, by which means their backs are to the circle, and their hands across their backs. They dance round in that form until the master calls 'Loose,' when they pass under the right sword, and are in a perfect circle.

"The master lays down his sword, and lays hold of the point of James's sword. He then turns himself, James, and the others, into a clew. When so formed, [the swords being held in a vaulted position], he passes under out of the midst of the circle; the others follow; they vault as before. After several other evolutions, [a repetition of all or part of the movements already described then ensues], they throw themselves into a circle, with their arms across the breast. They afterwards form such figures as to form a shield of their swords, and the shield is so compact that the master and his knights dance alternately with this shield upon their heads. It is then laid down upon the floor. Each knight lays hold of their former points and hilts [of the hilt and point which he before held] with their hands across [and placing his hands across his breast] which disentangle by figure directly contrary to those that formed the shield [extricates his sword from the shield by a figure directly opposite to that by which it had been formed]. This finishes the Ballet."

R. Willan's description of a West Yorkshire rapier-dance, referred to in Chapter II., on the word "rapper," may here for its valuable details be quoted nearly in full.

" At merry nights and on other festive occasions, they are introduced one after another by the names and titles of heroes . . . A spokesman then repeats some verses in praise of each, and they begin to flourish the rapier. On a signal given, all the weapons are united or interlaced, but soon withdrawn again, and brandished by the heroes, who exhibit great variety of evolutions, being usually accompanied by slow music.

" In the last scene, the Rapiers are united round the neck of a person kneeling in the centre, and when they are suddenly withdrawn, the victim falls to the ground; he is afterwards carried out, and a mock funeral is performed with pomp and solemn strains."

The text of a Durham sword-dancers' song and interlude (referred to above) is given by Bell in *Ballads and Songs of the Peasantry of England.* Unfortunately his description of the dance itself consists only of a few superficial observations on its ingenuity and the complexity of its figures.

The song is an introduction-song delivered by the Captain. The characters introduced are a Squire's Son, a Tailor, a Prodigal, a Skipper, a Jolly Dog, and the singer himself, whose "name it is True Blue." These are accompanied by a "Bessy," who is decorated with a hairy cap and a fox's brush dependent. Two more personages, a Parish Clergyman and a Doctor, appear in the interlude.

The song is followed by the dance, at the end of which " all the actors are seen fighting." The Parson intervenes and is killed. The interlude consists of his resuscitation by the " ten-pound Doctor," and concludes with a general dance.

A Wharfedale sword-song in the same collection introduces Captain Brown, Obadiah Trim the Tailor, a Foppish Knight, Love-ale the Vintner, and Bridget and Tom, the singer and his wife.

In Ellis's *Brand* (ed. 1849, i. 513), a brief account of
North Riding sword-dances from the *Gentleman's Magazine*
for May, 1811, is given.   Here the troupe consists of six
youths dressed in white with ribbons, a "Bessy" and a
Doctor.   A kind of farce is acted : the Bessy interferes while
they are making a hexagon with their swords, and is killed.
The Doctor's part is obvious, though not stated.

Wallis's mention of the sword-dance in his *History of
Northumberland* contains only one point of value—that the
chief character, who did not dance, generally wore a fox's
skin on his head, with the brush hanging down his
back.

Another song-text from Houghton-le-Spring is given by
Henderson (*Folk-Lore of the Northern Counties*, pp. 68-69).
The characters are King George, a Squire's Son, Little Foxey,
the King of Sicily and a Pitman.   These are accompanied
by two grotesques, the "Tommy" (singer of the song), who
wears a chintz dress with a belt, with a fox's head for a
cap, and the skin hanging below his shoulders, and the
"Bessy," clad in a woman's gown and a beaver hat.

The sword-play acted by the "Plow Boys or Morris
Dancers" at Revesby in Lincolnshire in 1779*, is a more
elaborate affair.   The characters are the Fool, his Five-Sons,
Pickle-Herring, Blue Breeches, Pepper Breeches, Ginger
Breeches, and Mr. Allspice—and one woman (acted by a man)
named Cicely.   Two of the actors double their parts as a
Hobby Horse and a Wild Worm, which make a transitory
appearance.   The action falls into two parts ; the death of
the Fool and the wooing of Cicely.   In the first the Fool,
after some primitive comedy, is killed by his sons "for his
estate."   In the second he comes to life again (without a
doctor's aid), immensely rejuvenated, competes with his sons,
who now appear as the Lord of Pool, the Knight of Lee and
so forth, for the love of the lady, and eventually carries
her off in triumph.   Several dances are interspersed in

---

* Text printed in *Folk Lore Journal*, vii. (1889), pp. 337-353.

the play, including "the Sword-Dance, which is called 'Nelly's Gig.'"

A foreign variant may end the list. This is a Harz-district sword-play, in which the sword-dance, though still present, is at a very low ebb. The characters are the Kings of England, Saxony, Poland, Denmark and Morocco; Hans, a servant; and Schnortison, the treasurer. The several introductions are made by the King of England in the usual stereotyped style. Last comes Schnortison, who is tried and condemned to death by the same king for rifling the collecting-box. The four other kings make a cross with their swords, upon which Schnortison steps: Hans hits him over the head with a wooden sword, and he falls for dead; he quickly, however, comes to life again, and the display ends with a round dance.

A comparison of the foregoing records with the descriptions of existing dances in this book will show that the sword-dance has altered little in the last four hundred years, and differs little locally, considering the wide area in which it has been found. Some of the features of the ancient dance have no doubt disappeared, and others have been modified, but many of its most typical figures have come down to us practically unaltered, and its essential unity runs through variants separated, in point of space, by half a continent.

Dancing in file or ring, linked hilt and point, is remarkably persistent from the earliest to the latest examples. Of the figures common to Kirkby and Grenoside "Your-Own-Sword" is found in the Ditmarschen and Shetland dances; "Single-Under" apparently in the Bacchu-Ber. The Grenoside "Reel" occurs in Ditmarschen. The Clash is as old as Olaus Magnus; so too is the increase of speed that marks the ending of the Grenoside dance.

But most persistent, striking and characteristic by far is the figure called variously the Rose, the Glass, the Shield, the Lock or the Nut (Knot). In all variants at all periods it occurs in some form. The method of tying it is not stated, the Shetland description alone suggesting a process similar to that of the Swalwell and Earsdon dancers.

It is variously applied. Sometimes one of the performers is hoisted on it, as at Nuremberg in 1600, and in Ditmarschen: sometimes crowned with it, as in the Shetland dance, where all in turn dance with it on their heads, and at Kirkby to day. Sometimes it is formed round someone's neck; so at Ulm, in the West Riding rapier-dance, in the Bacchu-Ber, at Grenoside and probably at Revesby, as will be shown presently.

It takes to itself a whole important section at the beginning of the Grenoside dance, forms the climax at Kirkby, and emerges as the end and aim of every figure in the Swalwell and Earsdon dances.

To the question of its significance we shall return.

Meanwhile the next salient point is the presence of drama in some degree, from its minimum in the mere song by one of the characters, introducing and naming the dancers, to its maximum in the elaborate play at Revesby. The dancers, even when they only dance, are yet personifications, bearing often some popular or local label—Squire's Son, Tailor, Skipper, Pitman and so forth — or a quaint appellation such as Little Foxey or the Jolly Dog. Where we find heroic figures—saints, as in the Shetland version ; kings, as in the Harz play ; or sometimes modern celebrities, as Wellington, Elliott or Nelson—literary influence is to be suspected. Perhaps even the spice-box nomenclature of the Revesby play is hardly of the folk. The Seven Champions at least must derive from the collection of their legends first published by Richard Johnson in 1596.

But the really essential point is that whenever this element of drama rises into the form of a play however rude, the central incident of this play is the death, or death and resurrection of one of the characters. In two examples this death is brought into direct relation with a special figure, the hexagon, Rose, or Lock. A detailed examination of the mummer's play is not within the scope of this volume : it must suffice to say that in all recorded versions, however degenerate, known to the writer, this death and resurrection of one of the characters is again the central incident. It is here that the sword shows itself the constant and indispensable property of the mumming play, and here too that the sword-dance in its dramatic element shows the closest affinity with it. But it is also on the dramatic side that the sword-dance, at least in the types of its *supernumerary* persons, is also in close touch with the Morris-dance.

In the sword-dances described in this volume, these characters vary between Captain alone at Grenoside, Captain and Fool at Kirkby, Captain and Bessy in both Tyneside dances; Bell's account gives Captain ("True Blue") and Bessy ; Henderson's, two grotesques, a Tommy and Bessy. Moreover that this pair (man and woman) is or has been the prevalent type, is shown by the fact that the sword-dancers in Northumberland not so long ago received (not from themselves) the general appellation of " the Tommies and Bessies." Now in the present-day Morris-dance the Fool or Squire is invariable (is the Squire's Son in two of the sword-dance versions a trace of the latter name?) and so until quite recently was a man-woman called the Moll, or occasionally Maid Marian. That these two have persisted together, in spite of the mating of the Woman sometimes with other characters, notably with the so-called Friar, and later with a Robin Hood intruded from ballad literature, seems to show that they have an essential relation to each other and an essential place in Morris customs. Fool and Woman are both seen in the Abbots Bromley dance ; a pair called King and Queen at Winster in Derbyshire : indeed the Lord and Lady or King and Queen, are so well known in festivals of this kind that it is useless to multiply instances.

As to the name Maid Marian, it may be suggested that Robin Hood, the popular ballad hero, intruding into seasonal festivals, as have other heroes, robbed some older character of his rights in the Moll or Malkin, whose name then took the literary form, under the influence perhaps of the old French *trouvère*-drama " Le Jeu de Robin et Marion," and she in her turn intrudes into the later form of the ballad-legend of Robin Hood.

In this pair of characters we have at least another very clear point of contact between the sword- and Morris-dances.

It now remains for us to see whether we can find anything in the sword-dance to indicate its derivation from one of the old nature-rites.

If such an indication exists, we should *primâ facie* expect to find it in the most conspicuous and characteristic figure of the dance, which is undoubtedly the figure in which the swords are interlaced. This, as above shown, is persistent in all recorded forms and has a most important place in the dances described in this book.

Now the meaning of this curious figure will be evident enough if we concentrate our attention on the Grenoside dance, where the incident is found perhaps in its most elaborate form. Here, I contend, only one interpretation is possible, namely, that it is a mimic decapitation. It would, indeed, be difficult to devise a more vivid representation of such a scene. We have the Captain with the swords interlaced about his neck, kneeling down in the midst of the ring. The dancers solemnly march or dance round him. At the climax of the figure they simultaneously and vigorously draw their swords across his neck ; there is a grinding clash of steel, and the Lock is disentangled. So realistic is the scene in actual performance, that when I first saw it I should not have been surprised if the Captain's head had toppled from his shoulders and rolled to the floor !

Moreover the semi-animalization of the Captain by the wearing of an animal's skin and head upon his helmet is so unmistakably a trait of primitive religion, that we need have no hesitation in seeing here not so much a mock execution as a mock sacrifice, reproducing in mimicry the slaughter of the victim in an old nature-rite.

But for the moment it is the interpretation of the figure as a death at all, that must occupy us. The strongest confirmation is that of the Rapier Dance noticed above. The same action is described in unmistakable terms, and then " a mock funeral " of the victim " is performed with pomp and solemn strains." Here at least there is hardly room for error.

Granting however that it is only in these two dances that our interpretation is irresistible, we can nevertheless, now that we possess the clue, glean some corroboration from other sources.

An examination of the text of the Revesby Play will, I think, reveal the fact that the Fool is there killed in the same way. The Lock seems to be formed three times in the course of the play. The first time it is expressly stated " they lock their swords to make the Glass," with which the Fool plays, finally throwing it down and jumping on it, whereupon it is disentangled. This is the signal for the announcement that he must die. He kneels down " with the swords round his neck " to say his last words. Finally the dancers " draw their swords, and the Fool falls on the floor."

Now whatever may be thought of the vague phrase, " with the swords round his neck," it is obvious that " draw their swords " does not mean the action of unsheathing, but of drawing their swords across his neck. The first attempt, however, is abortive : he must be killed over again : the swords are once more put round his neck ; the dancers sing:—

> " Good People all, I pray you now behold
> Our Old Fool's Bracelet is not made of Gold,
> But it is made of Iron and Good Steel "—

and this time the Fool falls dead. Is it too much to see in the collective term " Bracelet " applied to the swords at this point another name for the Lock ? And if the Lock is so used now, we may conclude it was so before. Taken apart from the Grenoside figure and the Rapier dance, this would be flimsy enough : with them it grows significant.

Again the Earsdon custom, now disused, of " hanging the Betty," as described hereafter (p. 82), seems to reproduce the same idea in a form very slightly different. But as striking support as any is derived from the record of a Spanish sword-dance (17th century), quoted by Müllenhoff,* one of the figures of which was called the *degollada* (beheadal) "because they encircle their leader's neck with the swords."

Let us admit that but for the evidence of the Grenoside dance, the Rapier dance, the *degollada*, and in a lesser degree of the Earsdon dance and the Revesby Play, it would have been fanciful indeed to see in the ordinary Rose figure any certain index of a mimic decapitation. A more probable explanation would have been the survival of some ancient coronation ceremony. For the locked swords placed on the head, as in the Shetland Islands and at Kirkby, might mean a crowning, but could not by any stretch of imagination be taken to indicate a beheadal. We may however fairly argue that, the meaning of the ceremony once forgotten, spectacular considerations might easily account for the change from shoulders to head, but it would be far harder to explain the reverse change from head to shoulders, had crowning been the original idea. As for the old variants in which someone is hoisted upon the swords, it is impossible to do more than hazard a conjecture. Those who prefer the crowning theory will see in it a parallel usage, the elevation of victor or king ; but if a sacrificial idea be admitted, it may at least be no less reasonably connected with the adoration of a divine victim not unknown in primitive rites.

And now it may be said, assuming that a killing is proved, all these instances point on the whole to the killing of a human victim : even the form of the figure itself suggests it :

---

* In a supplementary article, *Zeitschrift für deutsches Alterthum*, xviii., 11.

what then is the relation between such a sacrifice and the sacramental type, with an animal victim, discerned already in certain Morris-customs?

Now it was stated above that in the most primitive religions, the god, the clan, and the sacred animal were kinsmen. As a corollary animal life was as sacrosanct as that of the human clansman—even more so when the animal was regarded as mysteriously sharing in a divine life. To kill such a being for your own private use was murder of a heinous kind. Yet a holy animal might be killed (the whole clan taking the responsibility) for a sacramental purpose. Even so however the killing was very naturally a matter of a deep religious horror which impressed itself on the ceremonial. Time lapsed: animal life was no longer held so sacred as that of man, and possibly the idea of oblation was encroaching on that of sacrament. But ceremonial, always conservative, tenaciously maintaining the forms associated with the awfulness of the victim, led to a misconception. It was inferred that the original and perfect offering had been a man, for which the animal was a substitute; and thus grew up the custom of killing a human victim as a piacular sacrifice—a special sin offering in times of stress and peril—a return, as it was conceived, to the more perfect victim, which made atonement more certain. And now, as might be expected, the idea of oblation in such rites made great strides, while the sacramental idea receded. A further development was that of the occasional piacular sacrifice into an annual rite. It is such a sacrifice, in the mimic form to which time and civilization have reduced it, that we incline to see in the sword dance ceremony of the Lock.

To return to the ancient sacrifice in another aspect, we may remark that those tenacious ceremonies expressive of religious horror at the killing continued to be observed. Every sign of mourning and woe had preceded and accompanied the slaying of the animal-divine victim, and they still attended the slaughter of the human-divine. But the mourning was not of sorrow, but of fear—the dread of a community on the brink of an awful act. The deed done, and the atonement accomplished, the relieved worshippers, in a sudden revulsion of feeling, abandoned themselves to extravagant expressions of joy. But meanings were again forgotten: the mourning was interpreted as sorrow at the death of a deity, the revelry as joy that the divine was not really dead. And so arose a whole class of myths of gods dying and resurgent. And since the gods were nature powers, this death and resurrection in myth and ceremony was connected with the autumn death and spring birth of the world—annually the solemn and babarous rite shewed forth the yearly wax and wane of life, and was mystically identified with it. And now religion, in the minds of the simple, suffers the encroachment of an idea belonging strictly to primitive magic: the principle that the best means of producing an effect otherwise beyond man's control, is to give the best imitation humanly possible. The rite helped nature; nature was in a measure *dependent* on the rite. And so on this intrusive magical and mimetic footing, sacrifice and ceremony lingered on, the form outlived the reality of sacrifice—outlived, among simple folk, its meaning religious or magical, till we find its final shape in the death-scene and the doctor of the Mummers' Play.

And because the primitive mind drew no clear distinction between vegetable and animal fertility, and mating was an obvious symbol, we find in the old myths a god and goddess pair, we find the Fool carrying off Cicely at Revesby, the same character winning the Fair Lady in the Bassingbourne Christmas Play, and King and Queen, Lord and Lady, Squire and Moll, Tommy and Bessy, paired in festival after festival.

In Morris, sword-dance, and play we seem to intercept three stages of development, arrested and turned to its own uses by the civilized and social idea of entertainment: in the Oxford Morris-customs the earliest sacramental rite; in the sword-dance the later human sacrifice; in the mumming play the still later half-magical presentment of nature's annual death and renewal.

The trace of an animal victim in the rabbit-skin on the Grenoside captain's helmet, and the hairy cap of the formerly "hanged" Betty at Earsdon calls for a word. The animalization of a human victim is not unexampled in ancient rites; and stands on a different footing from the wearing of a skin by a worshipper either sacramentally or, later, to claim kinship with his god in presenting an offering. It was a frequent pious fraud to call an animal victim a man, on the erroneous supposition noted above that the latter was the more perfect victim. In the converse process perhaps we see a converse fraud—the worshipper attempting to hoodwink his own humanity, while suffering it to be overridden by his religious fears.

The connection of the Horn Dance with the other species of Morris-dance is now easy to see, and the points may be briefly enumerated. There are the six dancers carrying the horns which recall the sacramental wearing of the skin of the sacred and sacrificed animal, to secure the worshipper's participation in the divine life. The bow carried by the boy is the instrument of sacrifice, corresponding to the sword borne elsewhere before the Morris-dancers. A similar bow, if confirmation be needed, is found in a modern Thracian mumming play,* in which one of the actors (some of whom wear hairy caps) is killed with it. Fool, Woman and Hobby Horse also appear in the Horn Dance. The latter grotesque was a constant companion of the Morris-dancers of old time : at Winster it has only recently disappeared : in Kent too, until a few years ago, it was associated with the mummers, under the name of the Hooden Horse.

Lastly we have indications of the religious origin of the dance in the circular and serpentine character of its figures. These characteristic movements are to be found in nearly

---

* R. M. Dawkins in *Journal of Hellenic Studies*, xxvi. (1906), pp. 191-206.

all dances of a religious type. Vestiges of them perhaps remain in the Morris figures known as the Hey and Whole or Half Rounds, while they form the basis of the movements in the Farandole, the Helston Furry Dance, and many of the processional forms of the Morris-dance, notably Morris Off.

We see then that in addition to the common name of " Morris " which they bear among the people, the same central idea permeates all the dances and customs we have discussed. Originally expressions of religious belief, in which the idea was as essential as the form, they have passed by various stages and along devious paths into the inspiriting dances and quaint dramas with which we are familiar. That the human instinct of play should draw on these ceremonies, as their meaning waned, for its material, is natural enough, seeing that in them it found, ready to hand, a vehicle of expression easily adapted to its purpose. Out of the debris of ancient faith and cult have issued three forms of folk-art, and as in speaking of the origin we suggested that they represented three distinct religious phases, so in their latter development they exhibit three distinct artistic types. In the Morris-dance proper we have a dance of grace and dignity, instinct with emotion gravely restrained in a manner not unsuggestive of its older significance ; full of complex co-ordinated rhythms of hand and foot, demanding the perfection of unstrained muscular control. In the mummers' play the feeling for drama, the world-old love of personification, has been the determining factor ; while in the sword - dance with its elaborate dexterity of evolution, its dramatic accompaniments of song and interlude, we find drama and dance combined. Yet it is no mere hybrid : the dance element at least has an admirable austerity that is all its own.

The theory of origins put forward in these papers is by no means universally accepted. Some for instance hold, with Sir Walter Scott, that the sword-dance was imported into Great Britain by the Scandinavians ; just as others maintain that the Morris-dance is derived from the Moors of Spain. There is no doubt some truth in the statement that the sword-dance is found chiefly in those parts of England where a strong Scandinavian strain exists, but traces of it have been found in Devonshire, Sussex and Hampshire, while from Lincolnshire, perhaps the most Scandinavian of English counties, the Revesby Play is the sole record I have so far seen. And again, does not this theory at bottom spring from an assumption that the dance is exclusively Scandinavian? But its wide distribution over Europe hits that assumption hard, especially its appearance (leaving out of account the contaminated sword-and-buckler form) in Southern France and Spain, where, by the way, Don Quixote saw it at Camacho's wedding, and had often seen it before, but never better done. Yet no one on this latter ground has attempted to attribute it to the Moors.

The arguments in favour of the Moorish origin of the Morris-dance are more plausible. There is for example the fact that the dance is to be found to this day on both sides of the Franco-Spanish border, and in a form remarkably like that of the present English dance. But this can be explained on the assumption of a common source: it is not necessary to postulate a Moorish or any other national origin.

Again the accepted derivation of "Morris" from Morisco is held to be a proof. Now in the absence of any satisfactory alternative suggestion we may accept this with equanimity. We need hardly take a long shot with Dr. Frazer* and suggest a derivation from the cognate forms Mars, Mamurius, Morrius (the latter that mythical king of Veii who was traditionally the founder of the Salii), even though Mars in his original character was a vegetation god, and the dance of the Salii, his priests, perhaps a nature-rite parallel to the Morris-dance.

Rather we will turn to the next argument, the blackened face, in which many see the Moorish influence so strongly

---

* *The Golden Bough* (2nd ed.) iii. p. 125.

represented. Even now in many parts of England (*e.g.*, South Worcestershire) the morris-men black their faces. The same custom has been traced in France, the Netherlands, Germany and other countries : it has been found also in the sword-dance and the mummers' play. Surely whether the usage is derived from some primitive religious notion of disguise, or from the custom of smearing the face with the beneficent ashes of the festival fire, it is more reasonable to suppose with Mr. E. K. Chambers* that " the faces were not blackened because the dancers represented Moors, but rather the dancers were thought to represent Moors because their faces were blackened." To-day we habitually call a man who blacks his face in order to be entertaining, a " nigger." " Moor " was our forefathers' equivalent. And as long as we retain this belief we can afford to be calm about the etymology.

* *The Mediæval Stage*, i., 199.

CHAPTER I.

THE LONG-SWORD DANCE.

Two varieties of the sword dance are found in England, the long-sword dance of Yorkshire, and the short-sword dance of Northumberland and Durham.

The two species differ in many important particulars; in the form of the dance; the number of the performers; the principle upon which the figures and evolutions are constructed; and in many matters of a technical nature. These differences, though numerous, are, however, superficial, not fundamental, and although in the tide of evolution they have drifted far apart, the two types still retain many characteristics that testify to their common origin.

In this chapter two examples of the long-sword dance will be described.

THE KIRKBY MALZEARD SWORD DANCE.

Kirkby Malzeard is a small country village in the West Riding, about six miles north of Ripon. The Kirkby men came prominently before the public in 1886 at the Ripon Millenary Pageant where their performances won for them the reputation of being the most skilful exponents of the dance in the neighbourhood. It was from Mr. D'arcy de Ferrars, the Master of the Pageant, that I first heard of them.

An interesting and picturesque description of the Kirkby dance, written by Mr. Keighley Snowden, appeared in *The London Magazine* for 1906; and the Captain's song may be found in "English County Songs," p. 16, with a note giving a description of the costumes worn by the dancers several years ago.

Performances of this dance used to be given annually between Christmas Eve and the New Year in Kirkby and the surrounding villages, but this practice has now been discontinued for some years. Usually the dancers performed in the streets, but sometimes they would dance indoors. On the two occasions they danced to me they first performed by the side of the village cross which, I gathered, was the place where they were accustomed to dance before setting forth on their rounds.

The leader told me that when the dance was finished and the Fool was going round with his collecting box it used to be their custom to keep the crowd amused by performing "Jolly Lads." This was a hybrid form of entertainment consisting of a series of athletic feats varied with dance figures. As one of the latter, called "The waves of the sea" is the same as "The Roll" in the second part of the Grenoside dance, it is possible that "Jolly Lads" may once have formed an integral part of the Kirkby dance. The survival of this curious dance movement in both of these villages is interesting, because it is the most characteristic figure of the well-known old English country-dance Trenchmore, noted in Playford's "Dancing Master" (2nd ed., p. 103).

Of the athletic feats in "Jolly Lads" I saw one example only, and that was executed in the following way. The leader, standing back to back with one of the dancers, stretched his arms backward over his head and placed his hands under the chin of the man behind him. After two or three swaying movements back and forth, the leader bent forward and threw his companion over his head, the latter turning a back somersault and alighting on his feet face to face with the leader.

Beginners are recommended to use sticks instead of swords; they are more easily manipulated, less expensive and less dangerous. Thin bamboo canes of the sort that are used for light curtain rods, or for "sticking" peas, will make very suitable weapons if cut to the right length and bound at one end with cord for a handle.

It is essential that the dance should be performed smoothly and easily and without any apparent fluster or excitement. Although the dancers are usually linked together, hilt and point, by their swords and are thus always close beside each other, the complicated movements should be made without any jostling. Economy of motion is therefore all important. Each dancer must at every moment know exactly whither he is bound and proceed to his destination along the shortest and most direct path.

When I first saw the dance performed, it looked to me to be one continuous movement. It was not until I had seen it repeated that I realised that it was really compounded of a series of distinct and separate figures, like beads on a string. There should, therefore, be no pauses or gaps between the figures nor, more particularly, between the movements of which they are composed. Every performer must know how to execute each figure from six different positions. Beginners are advised to study one figure at a time, and to master it thoroughly before they pass on to the next one.

Eight performers take part in the dance—the Captain, the Fool, and six dancers; and these are accompanied by a musician who plays an accordion.

COSTUME.

The dancers wear red flannel tunics, cut soldier fashion, and trimmed with white braid down the front, and round the collar and sleeves; white trousers, or overalls, with a red stripe, an inch or more wide, down the side of each leg;

brown canvas shoes ; and tightly-fitting cricket caps, quartered in red and white (*see* plate facing p. 51). Each dancer carries a sword ; the leader an ordinary military weapon, and the others swords forged by the village blacksmith. The blades of these are of steel, about twenty-five inches long by three-quarters of an inch wide, and fitted with round wooden handles, five and a-half inches in length, without guards.

The Captain wears a blue coat of flowered cloth, ordinary trousers and a peaked cap of white flannel. Nowadays, he has a sword, but he used to carry a drum, slung round his waist, upon which he accompanied the dance tune.

The Fool—now, alas ! no more—used to wear a cocked hat, or a white wide-wake, decorated with peacocks' feathers. He carried a money-box and was armed with a halberd with which he pressed back the crowd and prevented them from encroaching upon the dancers. He wore a dinner-bell and a fox's tail attached to the back buckle of his trousers, and he used to run about among the spectators crying out :—

> A fox's tail ! a fox's tail !
> It 's noo to be seen ;
> Although I go ragged and wear an old coat,
> Who knows but I'm loved by the Queen ?

The musician is dressed in his ordinary clothes.

THE MUSIC.

The tune to which this dance is usually, though not invariably, performed is a very striking variant of the traditional air, known as "Brighton Camp" or "The Girl I've left behind me." Another version of the same air was used, many years ago, by the sword dancers of Stillington (Yorks).

Fig. 1, The Clash, begins and ends with the first strain of the tune. During the rest of the performance the figures proceed independently of the music, which controls the steps and nothing else.

THE STEP.

The step to which all the figures, with the exception of Nos. 1 and 7, are performed, is a very simple one. It may be described as a kind of leisurely tramp, or jog-trot, not unlike that used by soldiers when they advance slowly at the double. The steps fall on the first and middle beats of each bar of the music, and it is imperative that the tramp of the feet should be clearly heard and should synchronise with the rhythm of the tune.

N.B.—In this and the following dances the expressions "half-turn," "whole-turn," etc., are to be interpreted thus:—

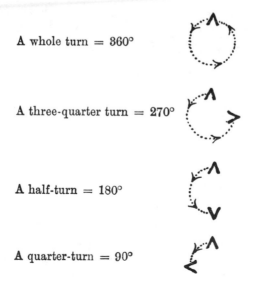

A whole turn = 360°

A three-quarter turn = 270°

A half-turn = 180°

A quarter-turn = 90°

THE DANCE.

The six dancers form up in line at right angles to the audience. The Captain stands about ten or twelve yards in front and faces them, thus :—

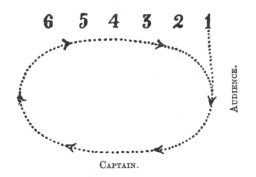

CAPTAIN.

The dancers stand at ease, resting the points of their swords on the ground, while the Captain, sword in hand, turns to the audience and sings the following song :—

i.   You noble spectators, wherever you be,
     Your attention I beg and I crave ;
     It 's all my desire you make a big room,
     And abundance of pastime you'll have.

ii. I am the second Sampson, in Judges you'll find,
     Who delights in his darling so dear ;
     What a blockhead was I for to tell her my mind
     So gallant and quick you shall hear.

iii. Here comes the man who laid hands upon me ;
     By him I was grieved to the heart.
     As I laid asleep on my dear darling's knee
     O the barber was playing his part.

iv. The second 's his brother, you might think they were
      twins,
    I thought by the world they would fight ;
    When these two Philistians seized on me,
    You 'd ha' thought they'd ha' ruined me quite.

v. The third is a man of so much milder blood,
    Some pity there 's lodged in his breast ;
    He oftentimes threatened to do me some good
    But he dursn't for fear of the rest.

vi. The fourth he comes on like a ranting young lad,
    He 's like to some majestial stands ;
    It was he that gave orders that I should be polled ;
    So they fettered my feet and my hands.

vii. The fifth is as cruel as cruel can be,
    The others and him did revise ;
    It was he that gave orders that I should no more see ;
    So they instantly bored out my eyes.

viii. The sixth is no better at all than the rest ;
    He was the first breeder of strife.
    If any of you there had been in my place,
    You'd been glad to com'd off with your life.

ix. These are the six lads that laid hands on me
    Without the consent of my dear ;
    But I will come even with them by and bye
    And so gallant and quick you shall hear.

x. When they were all merry carousing with wine
    The first one for Sampson did call ;
    He pulled down the house and slew all at that time ;
    So there was an end of them all.

xi. These here six actors bold
     Ne'er came on't stage before ;
     But they will do their best,
     And the best can do no more.

xii. You've seen them all go round ;
      Think on 'em what you will.
      Music ! strike up and play
      "T'aud wife of Dallowgill."

The first two stanzas are addressed to the audience. At the third stanza the Captain walks up to the leader, No. 1, and traces a scroll on the ground at his feet with the point of his sword. No. 1 then leaves the ranks and walks leisurely round in an oval track in front of the other dancers, as shown in the above diagram, dragging his sword on the ground.

At the beginning of the fourth stanza, the singer approaches No. 2 and traces a scroll on the ground at his feet. No. 2 then follows behind the leader, falling into position as the latter passes in front of him.

This procedure is repeated during the singing of the next four stanzas, so that on the conclusion of the eighth stanza the six dancers are marching, one behind the other, round the track.

The Captain then turns to the audience and sings to them the remaining lines of his song. At the words " Music ! strike up and play," the musician begins the dance air and the performance commences.

FIGURE 1.—THE CLASH.

The dancers move slowly round in a ring, clockwise, stepping in time with the music and clashing their swords together on the first and middle beats of each bar of the first strain of the music. The swords are held points up, hilts level with the chin, the blades, nearly vertical, forming a cone immediately above the centre of the circle.

Each dancer then places his sword over his left shoulder and grasps the sword-point belonging to the dancer in front of him. He then faces the centre of the ring, passes his sword over his head and lets his arms fall naturally to his sides. The dancers are now standing in a ring, facing centre, linked together by their swords, each one holding the hilt of his own sword in his right hand, and the tip of his left neighbour's sword in the other. Then, without pause, the following figures are performed.

It should be noted that the dancers remain linked together by their swords in the manner above described until the penultimate figure of the dance, which is the repetition of The Clash.

FIGURE 2.—SINGLE-UNDER.

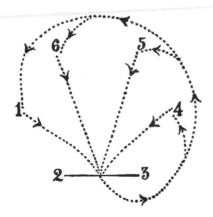

Nos. 2 and 3 face each other, raise the sword between them (No. 2's), and form an arch, under which No. 1, the leader, passes, followed, in order, by Nos. 6, 5 and 4. Immediately No. 1 has passed under the arch, he raises his right arm (see plate facing p. 46), turns to his left, passes outside No. 3, and, keeping his face towards the centre of the ring, dances back to his place, followed by Nos. 6, 5 and 4.

During this operation, No. 2 crosses his hands, left under right, raises his left wrist as high as possible, and walks a step or two away from the audience. As the movement is nearing its conclusion, he turns completely round on his axis, clockwise, and faces Nos. 3 and 4.

No. 3, immediately No. 4 has passed under the arch, makes a complete turn under his left arm, counter-clockwise, and faces centre.

The movement is then repeated five times in the manner above described, Nos. 2, 3, 4, 5 and 6, in turn, playing the part of leader and passing under arches formed, respectively, by Nos. 3 and 4, 4 and 5, 5 and 6, 6 and 1, and 1 and 2. This completes the figure.

The movement throughout should be continuous; there must be no pause or hesitation between the successive repetitions of the evolution. Each dancer will have, therefore, to bear in mind, not only the part he is playing at the moment, but the part he is to play in the succeeding repetition.

In practice it will be found unnecessary for the dancers to return to their original positions in the ring at the end of every movement. It will be enough if, after they have passed outside the circle, they proceed by the shortest path to the place from which they can most easily execute the next evolution.

Beginners will probably find that after each evolution the position of the ring has shifted in one direction or another. This tendency must be combated; it is imperative that the dancers should keep their ground and occupy the same area throughout the dance. This end will be achieved if the right upright (No. 3 in the initial movement of each figure), after executing his part in the movement, takes care to return to his original place.

KIRKBY-MALZEARD SWORD-DANCE
DOUBLE-UNDER. NOS. 1 AND 2 HAVE JUST PASSED UNDER THE ARCH *(see p. 50)*.

KIRKBY-MALZEARD SWORD-DANCE.
SINGLE-UNDER. NO 1 HAS JUST PASSED UNDER THE ARCH *(see p. 46)*.
Sword Dances.—Novello. D

FIGURE 3.—SINGLE-OVER.

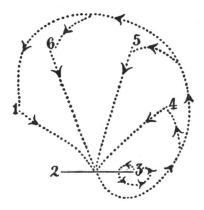

Nos. 2 and 3 face each other, stoop down, and hold the sword between them (No. 2's) from twelve to eighteen inches above, and parallel to the ground. The leader, No. 1, then jumps over the sword, raises his right arm, turns to his left, and, facing the centre of the ring, passes round No. 3 to his own place. He is followed, in order, by Nos. 6, 5 and 4, all of whom pass under No. 1's sword.

This movement, so far as Nos. 1, 6, 5 and 4 are concerned, is the same as in Single-Under, except that the performers leap over the sword instead of passing under it.

Directly No. 4 has jumped over the sword, No. 3 follows suit, turns to his left, counter-clockwise, and resumes his place, facing centre.

No. 2 then stands up and is ready to leap over the sword between Nos. 3 and 4.

As in the last figure, the evolution just described is repeated five times in succession, the dancers, led in turn by Nos. 2, 3, 4, 5 and 6, leaping the swords held by Nos. 3 and 4, 4 and 5, 5 and 6, 6 and 1, and 1 and 2.

On the completion of the last of these repetitions, Single-Under is performed.

FIGURE 4.—DOUBLE-SWORD.

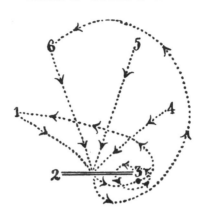

Nos. 2 and 3 face each other, stoop down, and hold the sword between them (No. 2's) as in Single-Over.

No. 1 then jumps over the sword, raises his left hand above his head, makes a quarter-turn clockwise, and stoops down close to and outside No. 3, placing his sword by the side of the other.   He then raises his left hand, *i.e.*, No. 6's sword, as high as possible, thus forming an arch between himself and No. 6.

No. 4 now jumps over the swords, turns to his left, passes round Nos. 3 and 1, and returns to his place, followed in succession by Nos. 5 and 6.   Nos. 4 and 5 pass under No. 6's sword.

To do this without breaking the ring, as soon as No. 4 has passed under No. 6's sword, No. 3 raises his right arm as high as possible and passes it over his head and round his left shoulder.

Immediately No. 6 has passed over the swords, No. 3 jumps over them.   Whereupon No. 1 stands up, makes a half turn counter-clockwise, and walks backwards to his place.   No. 3 immediately turns to his left and, following close behind

No. 1, returns to his place as in Single-Over; while No. 2 stands up, raises both arms and turns completely round on his axis counter-clockwise.

Double-Sword is a very complicated evolution and one, moreover, that is very difficult to perform neatly and, it may be added, to describe clearly in words. The crucial moment is directly after No. 6 has jumped over the swords, when all the dancers except No. 2 are standing close to each other. It will be found, however, that the strain at this point is relieved immediately No. 3, by jumping over the swords, frees his own right arm and No. 1's left. It will be well for beginners to practise the movement very slowly until they have thoroughly mastered its many difficulties.

As in the last two figures, the evolution is repeated five times, the dancers being led in turn by Nos. 2, 3, 4, 5 and 6.

This figure is followed by the performance of Single-Under.

FIGURE 5.—DOUBLE-UNDER.

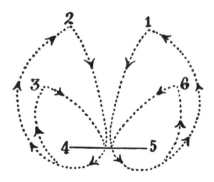

Nos. 1 and 2 advance, side by side, and pass under the sword held aloft by Nos. 4 and 5. No. 1 then raises his right arm, passes under his own sword, turns to his left round No. 5, and dances back to his place; while No. 2 raises his left arm and, passing under it, turns to his right and returns, round No. 4, to his place (*see* plate facing p. 46). Directly Nos. 1 and 2 have passed under the arch they should face each other, raise the sword between them (No. 1's) as high as possible, and pass it over the heads of the other four dancers.

Nos. 6 and 3, following close behind Nos. 1 and 2, then pass under the arch, side by side, and return to their places, No. 6 following No. 1, and No. 3 following No. 2.

Immediately Nos. 6 and 3 have passed under the arch, No. 4 turns completely round on his axis clockwise, and No. 5 does the same counter-clockwise.

This evolution is then repeated five times, the dancers passing successively under swords held up by Nos. 5 and 6, 6 and 1, 1 and 2, 2 and 3, and 3 and 4.

This completes the figure, which is followed, as in previous figures, by Single-Under.

FIGURE 6.—DOUBLE-OVER.

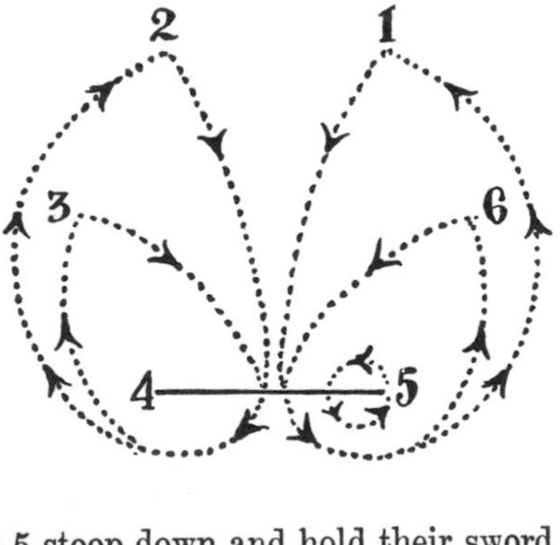

Nos. 4 and 5 stoop down and hold their sword as in Single-Over. Nos. 1 and 2 then advance, side by side, and leap

KIRKBY-MALZEARD SWORD-DANCE

DOUBLE-OVER.　　NOS. 1 AND 2 HAVE JUST JUMPED OVER THE SWORD (*see p. 51*).

over it (*see* plate facing p. 51), followed by Nos. 6 and 3, all
proceeding to their places as in Double-Under.

No. 5 then leaps over the sword, turns to his left and
resumes his place ; while No. 4 stands up in his own
place.

This movement is repeated five times, the dancers, in turn,
jumping over swords held successively by Nos. 5 and 6,
6 and 1, 1 and 2, 2 and 3, and 3 and 4.

On the completion of this figure Single-Under is executed.

Figure 7.—Your-Own-Sword.

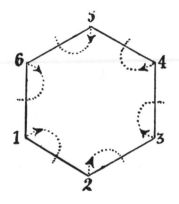

No. 1, raising his left hand above his head, faces No. 2
and jumps over his own sword, turns clockwise and faces
centre. Nos. 2, 3, 4, 5 and 6 then follow suit, each in turn
jumping over his own sword in the way above described.

Directly No. 6 has jumped over his own sword, Single-
under is performed without pause, on the completion of
which the dancers unlink left hands, follow one another
round in a ring and perform the Clash (Figure 1).

Figure 8.—The Lock.

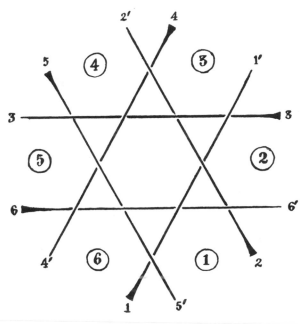

At the conclusion of the Clash the dancers, now linked together by their swords, draw close together, each crossing his right hand well over his left. Each man then drops the tip of his neighbour's sword and, using both his hands, presses the hilt of his own sword under the point of the sword adjacent to it, viz., No. 1's hilt under No. 5's point, No. 2's hilt under No. 6's point, and so forth. In this way the weapons are tightly and securely meshed together in the form of a double triangle, or six-pointed star, as shown in the above diagram. The process of fastening the swords together must be executed as quickly and smartly as possible.

The leader then grasps one of the hilts in his right hand and, raising the Lock high above his head, exhibits it to the spectators for a few moments. The Captain (formerly it was the Fool) then walks into the middle of the ring, where the Lock is placed on his head by the leader. This ceremony brings the dance to a conclusion.

NOTATION.

MOVEMENTS.

The Captain's song (*see* p. 42).
Fig. 1. The Clash (*see* p. 44).
Fig. 2. Single-Under (*see* p. 45).
Fig. 3. Single-Over (*see* p. 47).
Fig. 2. Single-Under.
Fig. 4. Double-Sword (*see* p. 48).
Fig. 2. Single-Under.
Fig. 5. Double-Under (*see* p. 49).
Fig. 2. Single-Under.
Fig. 6. Double-Over (*see* p. 50).
Fig. 2. Single-Under.
Fig. 7. Your-Own-Sword (*see* p. 51).
Fig. 2. Single-Under.
Fig. 1. The Clash.
Fig. 8. The Lock (*see* p. 52).

It has already been stated that the music controls the steps only and not the figures. It is impossible in the above notation, therefore, to give definite directions respecting the number of bars which the performance of each figure, except the first, should take. This will depend upon the temperament and skill of the dancers and the neatness with which they can execute the many twists and turns that occur in the various figures. And this, of course, is very largely a matter of practice. The important point to remember is that the whole dance, with the exception of the first and last figures, should be performed with the greatest spirit, without pause or hesitation, and at a speed at least as fast as that indicated in the music copy. The only quiet moments occur at the beginning and at the end of the dance.

THE GRENOSIDE SWORD DANCE.

GRENOSIDE, from whence the second example of the long-sword dance was derived, is a small hamlet in the West Riding, within an easy walk of Sheffield. The performers are miners who live in the village or in the neighbouring town of Ecclesfield. The performances used to take place annually on Christmas Eve and the following days, but of late years they have been discontinued owing, so I was told, to the indifference shown by the general public. Sometimes the dancers, after performing in their own village, would go round the country for two or three weeks, dancing in the villages and towns that they passed through, after the fashion of the Morris dancers at Whitsuntide in other parts of England. During the six or seven weeks immediately preceding Christmas, regular rehearsals used to be held two or three evenings a week, at which the younger and inexperienced dancers were instructed by the older men, a privilege for which they paid a few pence a week. This, again, is similar to the practice of the Morris men in the Midlands and Southern England.

The Grenoside men call themselves " Morris dancers," and explain the derivation of the term by saying that the dance originally came to them from the Moor lands further north.

An interesting and vivid account of the Grenoside dance was published in the *Pall Mall Gazette* of January 8th, 1885.

The performers are seven in number, the Captain and six dancers.

COSTUME.

The dancers wear loosely-fitting tunics of pink flowered calico, trimmed—back, front and sleeves—with blue and red braid, which is frilled and disposed in straight or waving lines, ovals, circles, &c. These designs, though similar in type, vary considerably in detail and in quantity ; as much as fifty or sixty yards of trimming are sometimes used in the decoration of a single tunic. The collar is of frilled braid, and small bows or rosettes of the same material are sewn on the coats wherever fancy dictates. The trousers are white overalls with a red stripe, an inch in width, down each leg. The small, tightly-fitting peaked caps are made of black velvet, with thin yellow stripes down the gores and a yellow button on the crown. The dancers wear clogs and carry swords similar to those of the Kirkby Malzeard men, the leader using a small cavalry sabre.

The Captain's dress is substantially the same as that worn by the dancers, except that perhaps his tunic is trimmed rather more lavishly. Instead of a cap, he wears a cloth helmet covered with a rabbit's skin, with the head of the animal set in front, surrounded with four bunches of coloured ribbons.

The musician plays an accordion and is dressed in his ordinary clothes.

THE MUSIC.

The dance is divided into two parts, separated by a short interval, and, unlike the Kirkby dance, it is always performed to the same tunes. Each figure and movement has its own proper music, and must be executed in a prescribed number of bars, in accordance with the directions given in the following descriptions and notation.

THE STEPS.

At certain places in the course of the dance the performers stand in position and " step," that is, dance a " double-shuffle " or a " break-down." This " stepping " was not executed in the same way by all the dancers ; but most of them danced a step which they adapted to the different measures in the following way:—

T.T. means a glancing stroke (something between a scrape and a tap), forwards and backwards, of the toe or ball of the foot. **T** indicates that the foot thus marked is to support the weight of the body.

In the evolutions, the performers simply walk, or rather tramp, in time with the music. The step is similar to that used in the Kirkby dance, but firmer and less elastic. This rhythmical tramping is one of the most characteristic features of the dance, and is especially noticeable, as well as extremely effective, in the concluding figure where the tempo is gradually increased to breakneck speed. It is for this reason, no doubt, that clogs are worn, and that the Grenoside men always prefer to dance indoors, in a kitchen or inn-parlour with a stone-flagged or sanded floor for choice.

THE DANCE.

The dancers arrange themselves in two rows, facing each other, thus :—

4>	*<3*
5>	*<2*
6>	*<1*

AUDIENCE.

No. 1 is the leader.

The Captain walks up and down between the files and sings the following song :—

i.   O ladies and gentlemen I'd have you make room,
Contented awhile for to be,
It is I and myself that has brought us along,
And my trade you will quickly see.

ii.   Whilst in foreign parts we rambled,
All both proper stout and tall,
Though we passed through many dangers
And at length we've caught a fall.

iii.   Wounded by a charming lady
Her charms I almost dread;
To die for her I am quite ready,
And at length I conquered her.

iv.   Six stout lads have I a-by me,
Both of honour and renown ;
Christmas time it 's growing nigher
And, since we've come in this town,

v.   Since that we have all come hither,
Fiddler, draw thy strings, advance !
Play beside us, here to guard us,
And these lads will show 'em a dance.

At the conclusion of his song the Captain moves away from between the files and the following figures are performed.

Figure 1.—Ring-and-Step.

The dancers walk round in a ring, clockwise, one behind the other. and march in time with the music, three steps to the bar. Each man places his sword horizontally over his left shoulder, and grasps the sword-point in front of him in his left hand and places it upon or close to his right shoulder. At the beginning of every bar of the music the swords are transferred from shoulder to shoulder ; that is, each man lifts his own sword over his head, say, from left shoulder to right, and the tip of his neighbour's sword from right shoulder to left, and so on (eight bars).

The dancers then turn inwards, face centre, and lower their arms to their sides, each man holding the hilt of his own sword in his right hand and the point of his left neighbour's sword in the other. In this position they stand still and " step " (eight bars).

Figure 2.—The Lock (A).

All turn outwards to the left, face in the opposite direction, and shouldering the swords as before, march round, counter-clockwise (eight bars). They again face centre and stand still in this position, linked together, but not " stepping." Whereupon the Captain moves into the middle of the ring and kneels down, the nearest pair of dancers raising the sword between them to admit him ; while the dancers form the Lock with their swords, in the way described in the previous dance, and place it round his neck (eight bars).

Figure 3.—The Lock (B).

The Captain stands up in the middle of the ring, and, holding the Lock in his right hand, raises it high above his head, while turning round very slowly, counter-clockwise ; at the same time, the dancers march round in the reverse direction (eight bars).

The Captain once again kneels down and places the Lock round his neck, the dancers marching round him clockwise (eight bars).

On the last beat of the final bar of the music, each man suddenly, and with great vigour, draws his own sword from the Lock ; the Captain slips out of the ring, the tune changes, the dancers quickly link themselves together with their swords, in the way previously described, and, without pause, proceed to perform Fig. 4.   The dancers remain linked together until the conclusion of the first part of the dance.

FIGURE 4.—SINGLE-SWORD-DANCING-ALL-THE-WAY-ROUND.

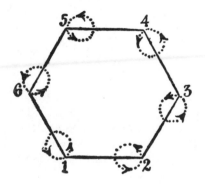

No. 6 lowers his sword on to the ground, while No. 1, raising his right arm, turns outward to his left and steps over the lowered sword, first with the right foot and then with the left, and faces centre, thus making a complete turn counter-clockwise.   He then immediately lowers his own sword, over which No. 2 steps in the same manner.

Nos. 3, 4, 5 and 6 follow suit in turn.   Each operation should be executed in one bar of the music ; so that the complete movement takes six bars to perform.   During the remaining two bars of the strain, the dancers stand in position and " step " (eight bars).

This evolution is then repeated five times, Nos. 2, 3, 4, 5 and 6 leading off in turn (forty-eight bars in all).

FIGURE 5.—SINGLE-SWORD-DOWN

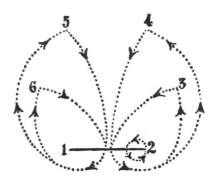

Nos. 1 and 2 stoop down and lower their sword (No. 1 s) to within an inch or two of the ground. The dancers then step over it in the following order, Nos. 5, 4, 6, 3. Nos. 5 and 6 turn to the right, pass round No. 1 and return to their places ; Nos. 4 and 3 turn to the left round No. 2 and dance back to their places.

No. 1 then steps over the sword and turns completely round on his axis, counter-clockwise ; while No. 1 stands up in his place (eight bars).

It will be seen that the movement is like that of Double-Over in the Kirkby dance, except that the dancers step instead of jumping over the sword, and pass over it singly instead of in pairs.

The evolution is then repeated five times over swords held in turn by Nos. 2 and 3, 3 and 4, 4 and 5, 5 and 6, 6 and 1. This completes the figure (forty-eight bars in all).

Figure 6.—Single-Sword-Up.

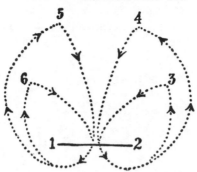

Nos. 1 and 2 make an arch with the sword between them (No. 1's), under which the rest of the dancers pass in the same way as in Single-Sword-Down. Nos. 1 and 2, however, instead of standing still turn their backs upon the audience, move a step or two forward, and turn completely round, each on his own axis, No. 1 clockwise and No. 2 counterclockwise (eight bars).

This evolution is repeated five times, the dancers passing under the swords raised in turn by Nos. 2 and 3, 3 and 4, 4 and 5, 5 and 6, and 6 and 1 (forty-eight bars in all).

Figure 7.—Double-Swords-Down.

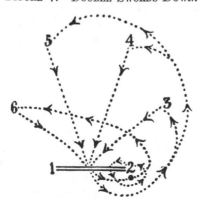

This figure is performed in the same way as Double-Sword in the Kirkby Malzeard dance, except that the swords are lowered nearer to the ground, and the dancers step instead of jump over them.

FIGURE 8.—DOUBLE-SWORDS-UP.

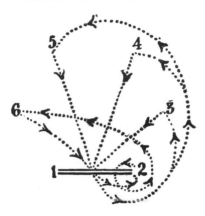

Nos. 1 and 2 make an arch with the sword between them (No. 1's). No. 6 then passes under it, turns under his right arm, faces No. 1, stands close to and outside No. 2, and makes a second arch with No. 1. Nos. 3, 4 and 5 in turn pass under the double arch, turn to the left and return to their places, Nos. 3 and 4 passing under No. 5's sword.

No. 2 then passes under the double arch and turns to his left, round No. 6, to position; No. 6, following close behind him, makes a half turn counter-clockwise and dances backward to his place; while No. 1 makes a complete turn on his axis, clockwise, and faces centre (eight bars).

This figure is, in principle, very much the same as Double-Swords-Down, except that, of course, the dancers pass under a double arch instead of over two swords. It will be seen, too, that No. 1, at the conclusion of the movement, turns clockwise and not counter-clockwise as in the previous figure.

The above evolution is (as usual) repeated five times (forty-eight bars in all).

This concludes the first part of the dance, between which and the second part there is a short interval.

PART II.

The six dancers stand in two rows facing each other, as at the beginning of Part I.

The Captain walks up and down between the files reciting the following lines :—

> Since that we have all come hither,
>
> And so sweetly I do sing,
>
> Now, my lads, you take to singing
>
> When you hear these swords to ring.

The Captain and his six men then sing " Tantiro " in chorus, still standing in the same position:—

> Tantiro, tantiro, the drums they do beat,
>
> The trumpets they do sound upon call;
>
> Methinks music's here, some bold Captain's near,
>
> March on ! my brave soldiers away.

On the conclusion of this song the Captain moves from between the files, and the following figures are danced :—

FIGURE 9.—THE REEL.

All form ring. Nos. 1, 3 and 5 face, respectively, Nos. 2, 4 and 6, thus:—

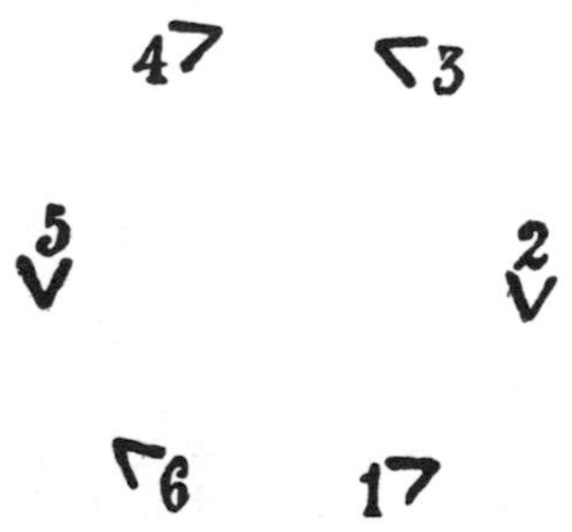

$$4^7 \qquad \vee 3$$

$$\overset{5}{\vee} \qquad\qquad \overset{2}{\vee}$$

$$\vee 6 \qquad 1^7$$

They then dance the Hey or Chain, with swords held vertically, points up, and hands breast-high. Nos. 1, 3 and 5 go round counter-clockwise, Nos. 2, 4 and 6 clockwise, passing each other, alternately, by the right and left shoulders. On the first beats of bars one, three, five and seven, that is, whenever the dancers are passing right shoulder to right shoulder, each pair clashes swords, moving them from right to left (eight bars).

They then form up in two lines, facing each other, and " step " (eight bars).

These two movements are then repeated (thirty-two bars in all).

FIGURE 10.—THE ROLL.

Standing in the same position, each dancer now takes hold of the sword-point of the man opposite to him with his left hand; so that each couple, Nos. 1 and 6, 2 and 5, and 3 and 4, is linked together by two parallel and horizontal swords, thus :—

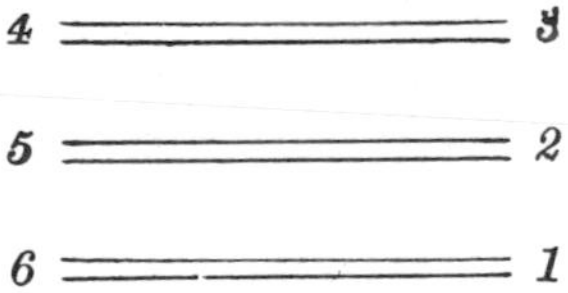

```
4 ================= 3

5 ================= 2

6 ================= 1
```

Nos. 1 and 6 then raise their swords and move down, exchanging places with Nos. 2 and 5, who move up under the swords held by Nos. 1 and 6.

Nos. 1 and 6 then stoop down, pass under the swords of Nos. 3 and 4 and exchange places with them. At the same moment Nos. 2 and 5 raise their arms and turn completely round, each on his own axis, No. 2 clockwise and No. 5 counter-clockwise.

This process is continued, each couple moving from one end to the other and back again, until all three couples are once again in their original places. At this point, if necessary the dancers pause a moment until the end of the fourth bar (four bars).

This movement is then repeated (four bars).

Partners should bear in mind that in moving up or down they must always pass *over* the middle couple and *under* the last couple—the top or bottom, as the case may be. The turn is made whenever a couple reaches the top or bottom position, and should occupy the same time as in passing under or over a couple.

The performers now release each other's swords, form up in two files, as before, and "step " (eight bars).

The Roll is then repeated twice, the tempo being gradually increased until the greatest possible speed has been attained (sixteen bars).

This is followed by the " stepping " as before, at the conclusion of which the dancers close in towards the centre of the ring, plant their right heels on the ground, toes up, hold their swords up above their heads, and remain posed in this position for a few moments, after the manner of the Morris All-In (eight bars).

NOTATION.

MUSIC.	MOVEMENTS.
	PART I.
Song.	Stand in two rows, facing (*see* p. 57).
THE JIG.	
A and B.	Fig. 1. Ring-and-Step (*see* p. 58).
A and B (2nd time).	Fig. 2. The Lock (A) (*see* p. 58).
A and B (3rd time).	Fig. 8. The Lock (B) (*see* p. 58).
THE HORNPIPE.	
C and D (3 times).	Fig. 4. Single-Sword-Dancing-All-The-Way-Round (*see* p. 59).
C and D (3 times).	Fig. 5. Single-Sword-Down (*see* p. 60).
C and D (3 times).	Fig. 6. Single-Sword-Up (*see* p. 61).
C and D (3 times).	Fig. 7. Double-Swords-Down (*see* p. 61).
C and D (3 times).	Fig. 8. Double-Swords-Up (*see* p. 62).
	INTERVAL.

NOTATION.

MUSIC.	MOVEMENTS.
	PART II.
The Captain's song.	Stand in two files, facing (*see* p. 63).
Chorus : Tantiro.	All sing Tantiro, standing in same position (*see* p. 63).
THE REEL.	
E and F.	Fig. 9. The Reel (*see* p. 63).
E and F (2nd time).	The same repeated.
THE ROLL.	
G and H.	Fig. 10. The Roll (*see* p. 64).
G and H (2nd time).	The Roll, increasing the tempo p. 65).
	ALL-IN.

CHAPTER II.

THE SHORT SWORD DANCE.

It is not easy to account for the substitution of the short sword, or rapper, for the long sword in the Northumberland and Durham sword dances; nor to determine at what period in the history of the dance the change was effected. The Captain of the Earsdon dancers, Mr. Armstrong, told me, on the authority of an old dancer who died many years ago at a great age, that the rapper was certainly used in his district at least a hundred years ago. Mr. Armstrong also added, on the same authority, that up to fifty years ago the rapper was fitted with two revolving handles, one at each end, so that there was no difference between hilt and point.

Now, the figures of the present Northumbrian dance cannot be executed with ordinary swords, or with any instruments less flexible than rappers, so that the introduction of the latter cannot have taken place at a later date than that of the present method of dancing.

But Brand, in his "Popular Antiquities of Great Britain" (1795), after quoting the description of the sword dance given by Olaus Magnus in his "History of the Northern Nations," makes the following comment: "I have been a frequent spectator of this dance, which is now, or was very lately, performed with few or no alterations in Northumberland and the adjoining counties." It will be remembered, however, that in the Scandinavian dance the performers "sheath their swords" and "hold them erect," and this, of course, they could not have done had they carried rappers. It is, at any rate, difficult to believe that Brand intended the words "few or no alterations" to cover such a vast and fundamental change in the form of the dance as the substitution of the rapper for the long sword would necessarily involve. It is reasonable, therefore, to conclude that the rapper had not been introduced into the Northumbrian dance when Brand saw it, *i.e.*, some time prior to 1795.

The evidence of Brand, who was an accurate and trustworthy observer, is, therefore, in direct conflict with the testimony of Mr. Armstrong. Unfortunately, I do not know of a single written description of a sword dance in which the use of the rapper is unmistakably implied, so that no assistance can be derived from printed sources.

The Yorkshire sword dance was, however, at one time known as the "rapier dance," for it is so described by R. Willan in his list of "Ancient words used in the West Riding of Yorkshire" (Archaeologia, 1814, vol. xvii., p. 155). But there is nothing in Willan's description of the dance to warrant the assumption that the flexible rapper was used in its performance.

The word "rapier" was introduced into this country in the 16th century and was originally used to denote a light and narrow cut-and-thrust weapon, as opposed to the heavy broad-sword. We may assume, moreover, that it was at first pronounced *rappier* or *rapper*, more probably the latter; just as the French *drapier* was in England pronounced *drapper* until about a century ago. There is no evidence, apparently, to show when the word became specialized in the sense in which it is now used in Northumberland and Durham.

There is a further point which presents some difficulty. The invention of the intricate bi-circle type of dance figure must have been the product of extraordinarily ingenious minds, and it is not easy, therefore, to explain its genesis by any theory of evolution. It would be easier to postulate the direct personal influence of some ingenious individual, and that at a comparatively late period in the history of the dance. The question is a very puzzling one, and I confess that, at present, I have no reasonable or satisfactory solution to offer.

The Northumberland and Durham dances, though extremely interesting, are, it seems to me, in a sense decadent. There is a kind of perverse ingenuity about them, a striving for effect in detail at the expense of broader features, which is very closely parallel to the rather tortured cleverness of art, or of literature, which has begun to go downhill. Markedly decadent, too, are the rappers, subordinated to the purposes of complex motion until they have lost nearly all the character of the sword. Again, what the dance gains in complexity, it loses in the closer massing of the men, due partly to the shortness of the rappers themselves. On the whole, therefore, the Yorkshire dances should, I think, be placed higher in artistic and traditional truth, in spite of the great fascination of the more elaborate figures of the Northumberland dances.

Whatever its origin and history there is no doubt that the rapper has now completely supplanted the sword in the Tyneside district. It is true that, like other forms of popular and traditional entertainment, short-sword dancing is rapidly dying out. But this is quite a recent phase. There is plenty of evidence to show that within the last ten years it was very generally practised in the neighbourhood of Newcastle-on-Tyne. So far, too, as my own investigations have gone, the dance itself seems to have varied but little. The number of figures that were performed in different villages varied very much, but in every case I noticed that the figures themselves had apparently been drawn from a common stock.

THE SWALWELL SWORD DANCE.

SWALWELL is a populous mining village within a few miles of
Newcastle, situated on the Durham bank of the Tyne. The
Swalwell sword dancers, or guizards as they are often called,
perform annually on Christmas Eve and on the following days.
Their performance differs from that at Earsdon and every
other village I investigated, in that it consists of the dance
only, without any acting or singing. I have been told,
however, that at one time the performance included the
usual introductory song by the Captain with its short
mummer-like sequel, both of which were very similar to
those presently to be described in the Earsdon dance. But
this must have been some time ago, for Mr. J. E. Taylor, a
resident in the neighbourhood, assures me that the form of
the dance has not materially changed within his recollection,
and his memory goes back a great many years.

The dancers are five in number, and are accompanied by a
Captain and a man dressed in woman's clothes, called the
Bessy, Betty, or dirty Bet, who carries a box and collects
the money.

COSTUME.

The dancers wear white shirts, decorated with red, white
and blue rosettes; a red tie, and a sash or belt of the same
colour round the waist; dark trousers, or, sometimes, white
overalls with a red stripe down each leg. They wear nothing
upon their heads. I am told that about fifty years ago,
instead of trousers they wore breeches and white stockings,
with ribbons tied round the knees.

The costumes of the Captain and the Bessy are shown in
the accompanying photograph.

SWALWELL SWORD-DANCERS,

WITH THE BETTY, MUSICIAN, CAPTAIN AND RAG-MAN

Each dancer carries a sword, twenty-eight inches in length, called a rapper. The blade, which is without a point, is made of thin, finely tempered steel, and is twenty-two inches long by one and three quarters wide. At one end a round wooden handle, six inches long, is loosely fitted so as to allow the metal haft, attached to the blade, to revolve freely within it ; upon each side of the other end two thin blocks of wood, two inches long and of the same width as the blade, are firmly rivetted or bound with cord. The rapper is as flexible as a harlequin's wand, to which in shape it bears some resemblance.

The musician, who is dressed in his ordinary clothes, plays a fiddle.

THE MUSIC.

There is no special or traditional air associated with this dance ; any jig tune in 6-8 time will serve, the dancers told me, so long as it can be played at the proper speed ($\downarrow \cdot = 160$).

THE STEPS.

Throughout the dance the performers stand very close to each other and step, or tramp, in time with the music, taking two short, decided, steps to each bar. At the end of every "Nut," as each section of the dance is called, the performers stand still and "step" as in the Grenoside dance.

THE DANCE.

The performers stand in a ring, facing centre, while the fiddler plays through the first strain of the music. On the last beat of the last, bar, they clash their swords together (as in the Kirkby dance), and then, taking a quarter turn to the left, each man throws his rapper over his left shoulder and grasps the tip of the sword in front of him. In this position they march round in a ring, clockwise (eight bars), and then, without pause, break into the following figure:—

FIGURE 1.—ONE-TURN-OFF.

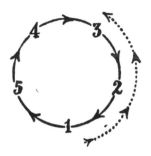

Nos. 2, 3, 4 and 5 continue to move round, clockwise, while No. 1, the leader, raises both arms, turns outward to his left, and dances round and outside the ring counter-clockwise, until he comes to his own place, when he turns in and resumes his original position behind No. 5.

The movement is then repeated four times, Nos. 2, 3, 4 and 5, in turn, dancing round and outside the ring in the same way.

FIGURE 2.—THE NUT.

No. 1 raises his left arm, turns outward to his left and moves round a half circle counter-clockwise, followed by Nos. 2, 3 and 4, all of whom pass under No. 5's sword. Simultaneously, No. 5, raising his right arm and keeping his face towards the centre, moves round the ring, clockwise, until he meets No. 1 (*see* plate facing p. 75).

A new ring is thus formed, in which the dancers are

SWALWELL SWORD-DANCE.

THE DANCERS ARE ABOUT TO TIE THE NUT *(see p. 74)*. THE LEADER, NO. 1, IS ON THE EXTREME RIGHT, AND IS PREPARING TO TURN OUTWARDS TO HIS LEFT. READING FROM RIGHT TO LEFT THE DANCERS ARE STANDING IN THE FOLLOWING ORDER: NOS. 1, 2, 3, 4 AND 5.

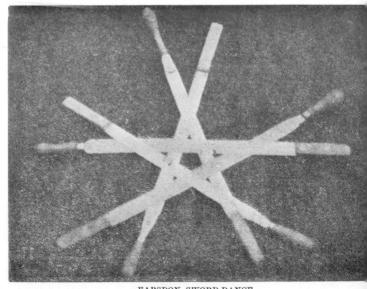

EARSDON SWORD-DANCE
THE NUT *(see p. 75)*.

standing in reversed order, as shown in the following
diagram :—

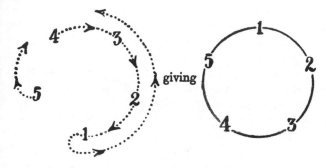

The dancers, keeping their wrists raised to chin level, press
their hands apart, each man passing his right hand *under* the
left wrist of the dancer on his right, and his left hand *over*
the right wrist of the man on his left.   In this way the
swords are locked together in the form of a pentacle or five-
pointed star (*see* plate facing p. 75).   This is called the
" Nut " or " Knot."

The leader then raises the Nut in his right hand and holds
it high above his head, while all five dancers walk round in a
ring clockwise, two steps to the bar, each one placing his left
arm upon the left shoulder of the man in front of him
(8 bars).

They now halt, face centre, and " step " while they hold up
the Nut, in a horizontal position, well above their heads
(eight bars), as shown in the frontispiece.   The Nut is supported
by all the dancers, each of whom grasps the hilt of his own
sword in his right hand, and the tip of his right neighbour's
sword in the other.

The Nut is then untied by reversing the movement by
which the swords were interlaced.   That is to say, No. 1
raises both arms, turns outward to his right and moves round
clockwise to his place, followed by Nos. 2, 3 and 4, all of
whom pass under No. 5's sword ; while No. 5 raises his

right arm, moves round counter-clockwise, facing centre, and meets No. 1.

The dancers are now standing in a ring, facing centre, and linked together, hilt and point, as in the Yorkshire long-sword dances. This is the normal position in which the dancers should stand at the beginning and end of the figures in this and the following dance. To this rule there is but one exception, viz., in One-Turn-Off, which, as already explained, the dancers begin and end holding their rappers over their left shoulders. This position, moreover, is maintained at the end of this figure only when it is followed by the tying of the Nut; and that occurs once only in the course of the dance. On all other occasions the dancers at the conclusion of Fig. 1 pass their rappers over their heads, make a quarter turn clockwise and face centre.

This completes the first of the four sections into which this dance is divided. The first section, or Nut, as it is usually called, consists, as we have seen, of One-Turn-Off and the Nut. Each of the succeeding Nuts begins with Fig. 1 and ends with Fig. 2, and contains, in addition, a third figure interposed between them.

The division of the dance into sections is purely arbitrary, and is done for the sake of convenience and clearness. The movements of the performers throughout the dance are continuous, no pause being made between the successive Nuts, or between the figures of which they are composed. Immediately, therefore, one Nut is finished, the dancers break, without hesitation, into One-Turn-Off, which is always the first figure of the next section.

When a figure, as is usually the case, consists of several repetitions of a movement, the number of such repetitions is determined by the leader, whose privilege it is to call " Nut " and to break into Fig. 2 whenever he thinks fit. He must, however, be careful to time his call so that the tying of the

Nut shall coincide with the end of one strain of the tune. As the two following movements take exactly sixteen bars to perform, each section of the dance, or Nut, will thus begin and end with the first and last bars of one or other of the strains of the music.

In the third and fourth figures of this dance (and in many of those in the Earsdon dance) the Nut is tied in a different way from that described in Fig. 2. In such cases the special method will always be explained at the end of the figure in which it occurs.

The distinctive figures of the remaining three Nuts will now be described in their proper order.

FIGURE 3.—THE NEEDLE.

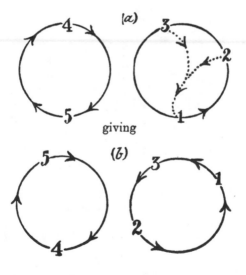

No. 1 raises his left arm, turns outward to his left and, followed by Nos. 2 and 3, moves round in a circle counter-clockwise. Simultaneously, No. 5 raises his right arm, turns outward to his right and, followed by No. 4, moves round in a circle clockwise (*see* diagram *a*).

The dancers are now moving round in two circles, like cog-wheels, at the same rate, but in opposite directions, Nos. 1, 2 and 3 counter-clockwise, and Nos. 5 and 4 clockwise (*see* diagram *b*).

At the beginning of every fresh circuit No. 3 crosses over from one circle to the other, and dances, therefore, in successive circuits, alternately behind No. 2 and No. 4, as shown in the following diagrams :—

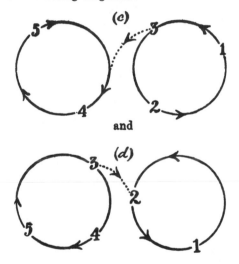

The leader must be careful to call " Nut " only when No. 3 is just entering the right-hand circle, and is about to follow behind No. 2 (*see* diagram *d*). No. 1 then continues moving round, counter-clockwise, followed by Nos. 2, 3 and 4 ; while No. 5 moves forward a step or two, makes a three-quarter turn counter-clockwise and faces centre.

In this and in all figures in which the performers are moving round in adjacent circles, it will be necessary for the dancers to keep their hands well above their heads.

FIGURE 4.—RIGHT-AND-LEFT.

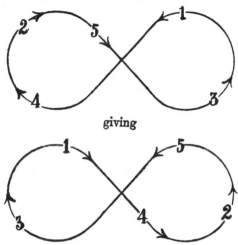

giving

No. 1 raises his left hand, turns outward to his left and, followed by No. 3, moves round in a circle counter-clockwise; while No. 5, raising his right arm, turns outward to his right and, followed by Nos. 2 and 4, moves round in a circle clockwise.

At the end of every circuit, each group of dancers crosses over from one circle to the other and moves round in the reverse direction. The track, therefore, described by the dancers is, roughly, the figure 8, by which name this figure is sometimes called.

The critical moment is when the two groups meet, face to face, at the junction between the loops. The crossing at this point is executed in the following order, Nos. 5, 1, 2, 3, 4.

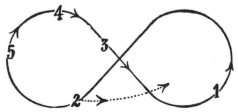

The Nut can only be tied when No. 1 is in the right-hand circle and No. 2 has just crossed over into the left-hand circle, the dancers then being in the positions shown in the above diagram.   No. 2 then crosses over between Nos. 1 and 3; whereupon No. 1, followed by Nos. 2, 3 and 4, moves round counter-clockwise and ties the Nut in the usual manner, No. 5 making a three-quarter turn counter-clockwise and facing centre.

Figure 5.—Rank.

All face centre and move round clockwise until No. 1 is facing audience, thus :—

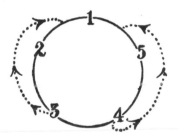

No. 3 raises both hands and, facing centre, moves to his left; he passes behind No. 2, stands between Nos. 1 and 2, and faces the audience.   Simultaneously No. 4, raising his left arm, turns outward to his left, passes behind No. 5, stands between Nos. 1 and 5, and faces the audience.

The dancers are now standing in line, facing the audience, in the following order (*see* plate facing p. 80) :—

2   3   1   4   5

At the beginning of the next strain of the music, Nos. 1 and 2, and Nos. 1 and 5 lower the swords between them (No. 1's and No. 5's), over which Nos. 3 and 4, respectively,

SWALWELL SWORD-DANCE. RANK (*see p.* 90).

jump. In this position all "step" to the end of the strain (eight bars).

The same swords are again lowered and Nos. 3 and 4 jump backwards over them into their places in the line; after which all "step" till the end of the strain (eight bars).

Nos. 3 and 4 now lower the sword between them (No. 3's) and No. 1 leaps over it. Then all "step" till the end of the strain, when No. 1 jumps backwards over it into his place (eight bars).

The Nut is then tied in the following way: No. 1, raising both arms, moves forward, passes under No. 3's sword and makes a half turn counter-clockwise; while No. 5 turns completely round on his axis counter-clockwise.

———

On completing the last Nut, the dancers form up in line, facing audience. No. 1 stands in the middle and holds up the Nut high above his head in his right hand. This brings the dance to a conclusion.

NOTATION.

MOVEMENTS.

Clash swords and march round in a ring (*see* p. 73).

Fig. 1.   One-Turn-Off (*see* p. 74).
Fig. 2.   The Nut (*see* p. 74).
Fig. 1.   One-Turn-Off.
Fig. 3.   The Needle (*see* p. 77).
Fig. 2.   The Nut.
Fig. 1.   One-Turn-Off.
Fig. 4.   Right-and-Left (*see* p. 79).
Fig. 2.   The Nut.
Fig. 1.   One-Turn-Off.
Fig. 5.   Rank (*see* p. 80).
Fig. 2.   The Nut.

Form up in line end exhibit Nut (*see* p. 81).

THE EARSDON SWORD DANCE.

THE Earsdon guizards perform in public on Christmas Eve, and they hold the reputation of being the best sword dancers in Northumberland.

Mr. Armstrong, the Captain, danced with them for forty years before he retired and took his present position. He told me that old-fashioned people always call them "Morris dancers." He explained the derivation of the expression by saying that the dance was originally brought to the Border country by bands of outlaws and sheep-stealers, called "Morris (Moss) troopers," who came from the North and settled down as miners in Northumbria.

As Mr. Armstrong's memory goes back a long way, he was able to give me a good deal of information respecting the changes that have taken place in the dance during the last fifty years. The Bessy, for instance, used to wear a hairy cap, and when the Nut was about to be tied the dancers would sometimes call out "We'll hang the Betty"; whereupon, Betty would step into the centre of the ring and the swords would be locked tightly around his throat, while the dancers "stepped" in the way described in the text. Mr. Armstrong also sang to me an older version of the Captain's song and gave me the words of the dramatic interlude which used to follow it. As these are of great interest they will be printed together with the version at present used.

The performers are a Captain, a Bessy, and five dancers. They are accompanied by a musician, who plays a fiddle.

COSTUME.

The costume which the dancers at present wear is a very elaborate one: crimson plush breeches, white linen shirts, a Zouave jacket of crimson plush edged with gold braid, and a broad Toreador sash. The Captain's dress is the same as that of the dancers with the addition of a cocked hat lavishly trimmed with gold lace (*see* plate facing p. 97).

This elaborate and gorgeous costume is quite a recent innovation and was adopted only a few years ago when the dancers were invited to Alnwick Castle to perform before the late King.

The older and traditional dress is shown in the frontispiece, which is a reproduction of a picture painted about thirty years ago by Mr. Ralph Hedley. At that time, Mr. Hedley assures me, the dancers wore white shirts decorated with bows and rosettes of coloured ribbons, black breeches of alpaca or satinet, knee-ribbons and striped stockings and shoes tied with ribbons. The Captain wore a wide-awake hat with peacocks' feathers, an old-fashioned tail coat, breeches, and striped stockings. The Bessy was dressed in woman's clothes as shown in the picture.

The Earsdon dancers carry rappers similar to, but more neatly made and better finished than those used by the Swalwell men. The blades measure twenty-four inches in length, by one and an eighth in width.

THE MUSIC.

The music is supplied by a fiddler who is dressed in his ordinary clothes. As there is no special traditional tune to the dance any jig in 6-8 time is used that can be played at the required speed (M.M. $\downarrow$. =160). When they were good enough to dance to me the fiddler played " The Threepenny Bit " for the first half of the dance and " The Black-thorn Stick " during the later figures. Their most popular tunes appear to be "The Laird o' Cockpen," "The Irish Washerwoman," "Haste to the Wedding," "The Delight," " Paddy O'Rafferty " and "Kitty's Ramble."

THE STEPS.

The steps are exactly the same as those used in the Swalwell dance.

THE DANCE.

The performance, as is usual with sword dances, opens with the Captain's song, followed by a few introductory movements leading up to the dance proper, which begins with Figure 1. This introduction, as has been already explained, has undergone some alteration in the course of the last few years. Both versions, old and modern, will therefore be given.

INTRODUCTION.
(OLD VERSION.)

The dancers stand in line, facing the audience, while the Captain walks round in a circle counter-clockwise, thus:—

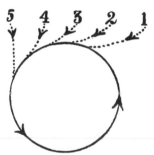

In the course of the following song, the dancers, as they are introduced, leave the line, one by one, and fall in and walk behind the Captain.

THE CAPTAIN'S SONG.

i.   A-rambling here I've comed,
Good people for to see ;
Five actors I have brought,
As brave as brave can be.

ii.   It's Earsdon on the hill,
Where the water washes clear ;
To Earsdon habitation we belong,
And merry we'll appear.

iii. The first that I'll call on,
He is a pitman bold;
He walks on underground
To keep him from the cold.

iv. The next that I'll call on,
It is his heart's desire
He hews and puts the coals,
The old woman makes the fire.

v. The next that I'll call on,
He is a tailor fine.
What think you of his work?
He made this coat of mine.

vi. He is a tailor fine,
And a good one to his trade;
He never closed one hole
But two for one he made.

vii. The next that I'll call on,
Is Jack upon the deck;
He cooks for our ship's crew
And he sells all the fat.

viii. The next that I'll call on,
It is big walloping Tom;
He's courted two fair women
And durst not marry one.

ix. For if he married one,
The other he would slight;
And the best thing he can do
Is to treat them both alike.

x. Now I'm going to kill a bullock,
Of that I'll make you sure;
We'll kill it in Earsdon Town
And divide it amongst the poor.

Directly this song is finished, two of the dancers, Nos. 1 and 2, feigning a quarrel, fight with their swords until one of them is wounded and falls to the ground. Whereupon there is a great commotion and Bessy sings :—

> An actor he is dead,
> And on the ground he's laid ;
> We'll have to suffer for it,
> Brave boys, I'm sore afraid.

No. 3 then sings :—

> I'm sure it's none of me,
> And never in my time ;
> It's he that followed I,
> That did this bloody crime.

Then No. 4 interposes :—

> O, now that he is dead
> And his body it is cold,
> We'll take him to the Church yard
> And bury him in the mould.

The following dialogue then takes place :—

No. 5. Doctor ! doctor ! O, for a ten-pound doctor !

Doctor (*enters*). Here am I !

No. 5. How came you to be a doctor ?

Doctor. By my travels.

No. 5. How far have you travelled ?

Doctor. Through Italy, France and Spain ; and now I've come back to cure the diseases in England again. Jack ! take a drop of my little bottle, that'll go down your thrittle throttle. Rise up ! and fight for old England again.

The wounded man then stands up and shakes his sword ; whereupon Bessy sings :—

> Dance on, my bonny lads,
> I heard the landlord say
> He would stand a gallon of beer
> Before we go away.

The dancers then form up in line, facing audience, and the dance proceeds in the way described at p. 89.

INTRODUCTION

(MODERN VERSION.)

The dancers stand in line, facing the audience, each with his sword resting upon his right shoulder, the hilt level with his waist. The Captain and Betty stand at either end of the line, thus :—

Captain. *5. 4. 3. 2. 1.* Betty.

The song, which follows, should be sung by the Captain; nowadays, however, Bessie, being the younger man, usually sings it in his stead.

THE CAPTAIN'S SONG.

i.

Good people, give ear to my story, we have called for to see you by chance;

Five heroes I've brought blithe and bonny, intending to give you a dance.

For Earsdon is our habitation, the place we were all born and bred.

There are not finer boys in the nation, and none shall be more gallantly led.

ii.

'Tis not for your gold or your silver, nor yet for the gain of your gear,

But we come just to take a week's pleasure, to welcome the incoming year.

My lads, they are all fit for action, with spirits and courage so bold;

They are born of a noble extraction, their fathers were heroes of old.

iii.

Now this is the son of brave Elliott, the first youth that
enters my ring;
So proudly rejoice I to tell it, he fought for his country and
king.
When the Spaniards besieged Gibraltar, bold Elliott defended
the place,
Soon caused them their plans for to alter; some died—others
fell in disgrace.

iv.

Now my next handsome youth that does enter is a boy, there
are very few such;
His father beat that great De Winter, and defeated the fleet
of the Dutch.
His father was the great Lord Duncan, who played the Dutch
ne'er such a prank,
That they fled from their harbours, ran funkin', and they fled
to the great Dogger Bank.

v.

This one is the son of Lord Nelson, that hero that fought at
the Nile;
Few men with such courage and talent, the Frenchmen he
did them beguile.
The Frenchmen they nearly decoyed him, but the battle he
managed so well,
In their fortress he wholly destroyed them, scarce one got
home for to tell.

vi.

Now my next handsome youth that does enter is a boy of
ability bright;
Five thousand gold guineas I'd venture that he like his father
would fight.
At Waterloo and Tarryvary, Lord Wellington made the
French fly;
You scarcely can find such another, he'd conquer or else he
would die.

vii.

Now my last handsome youth that does enter is a boy that is
both straight and tall;

He is the son of the great Buonaparte, the hero that cracked
the whole all.

He went over the Lowlands like thunder, made nations to
quiver and quake;

Many thousands stood gazing in wonder at the havoc he
always did make.

viii.

Now you see all my five noble heroes, my five noble heroes
by birth,

And they each bear as good a character as any five heroes
on earth;

If they be as good as their fathers, their deeds are deserving
records;

It is all the whole company desires to see how they handle
their swords.

At the end of each stanza, the singer pauses for a moment
while the dancers clash their swords together, Nos. 5 and 4
and Nos. 1 and 2 moving towards each other so as to get
within reach.

At the beginning of the third stanza, No. 1 moves forward
two paces and remains there until the end of the song. In
the four following stanzas Nos. 2, 3, 4 and 5, respectively,
follow suit.

Directly the song is finished, the fiddler strikes up, the
dancers form a ring, one behind the other, hold their swords
points up, hilts breast high, and place their left arms over
the left shoulders of those in front of them. Standing in this
position they " step " (eight bars).

On the last beat of the last bar they clash their swords
together and place them on their left shoulders, each man
grasping in his left hand the tip of the sword in front of him.

In this position they forthwith break into the following figure without pause.

FIGURE 1.—SINGLE-GUARD.

This is danced in exactly the same way as One-Turn-Off (*see* p. 74).

FIGURE 2.—THE NUT.

This figure begins with the tying of the Nut, which is done in precisely the same way as in the Swalwell dance (*see* p. 74).

The dancers then form up in line, facing the audience, and "step," the leader in the middle holding the Nut in his right hand high up above his head (eight bars).

They then form ring, facing centre, and raise the Nut above their heads, in a horizontal position (*see* frontispiece), each man holding the hilt of his own sword in his right hand, and the tip of his right neighbour's sword in the other. In this position they "step" (eight bars).

On the last beat of the last bar they lower the Nut and "break-away," that is, they loosen the swords with a sharp jerk of the wrists downwards and towards each other, and then proceed to untie the Nut in the following way.

No. 1 stands still and raises his right arm. No. 2, followed by Nos. 3, 4 and 5, then turns outward to his right and, passing under No. 1's sword, moves round in a circle, counter-clockwise, until he meets No. 1, when all stand still, make a quarter turn to the right and face centre, thus :—

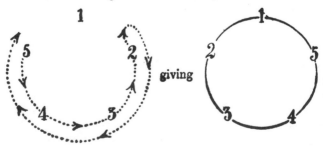

This movement, it will be noticed, differs from that described in the Swalwell dance. The latter is, of course, the more logical way because, in principle, it accords with the method in which the Nut was tied. The Earsdon men told me that they acquired their present habit some years ago when they had a leader who was an old man and it was necessary to do all that they could to spare him trouble. It is curious that, this being their object, they did not lighten his labour still further by tying the Nut on the same principle, thus :—

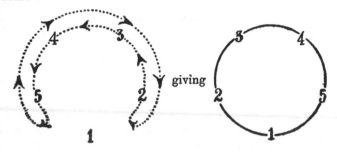

giving

This brings the first Nut to a conclusion. The construction of the rest of the dance is the same as that of the Swalwell dance, and consists of a series of Nuts, each of which begins and ends, respectively, with the two figures above described, and contains, interposed between them, a new and additional figure. The order in which these special figures are presented is not prescribed, but is determined by the leader, who calls out the name of the next figure during the performance of Single-guard. As in the Swalwell dance, whenever the Nut is tied in any other than the normal way, this will be specifically mentioned and described at the end of each figure in which it occurs.

The distinctive figures will now be described in their proper order.

Figure 3.—Three-and-Two.

This is the same figure as the Needle (*see* p. 77).

Figure 4.—Turn-In.

This is a variant of Single-Guard.

Raising both arms, the dancers make a three-quarter turn, clockwise, and then proceed to move round in a circle in the same direction, one behind the other.

No. 1 then raises both arms, moves a step outside the ring, revolves twice on his axis counter-clockwise, and then dances round and outside the circle counter-clockwise until he comes to his place, when he turns in, as in Single-Guard.

This evolution is then executed, successively, by Nos. 2, 3, 4 and 5. Immediately No. 5 has resumed his place, No. 1 turns outward and the Nut is tied in the usual manner.

Figure 5.—Follow-We.

No. 1 raises his left arm and, followed by Nos. 2, 3 and 4, moves round in a circle counter-clockwise; while No. 5, raising his right arm, turns out to his right and goes round in a circle, clockwise, by himself.

At the end of the first circuit, No. 2 leaves the right-hand circle and follows behind No. 5.

At the end of the second and third circuits, Nos. 3 and 4, respectively, join No. 5's circle.

This evolution is now executed in the reverse way, Nos. 2, 3 and 4, successively leaving the left for the right-hand circle.

The figure may be repeated as often as the leader wishes. The Nut, however, can only be tied when No. 2 is entering the right-hand circle.

Figure 6.—Changy.

This is a variant of Three-and-Two.

No. 1 raises his left arm, turns outward to his left and, followed by Nos. 2 and 3, moves round in a circle counter-clockwise. Simultaneously, No. 5 raises his right arm, turns outward to his right and, followed by No. 4, goes round in a circle clockwise.

At the end of every circuit, Nos. 1 and 5 change places, No. 5 always passing *in front* of No. 1.

The Nut can be tied in the usual way whenever No. 1 is entering the right-hand circle. No. 5, however, must be careful to face centre by turning counter-clockwise.

FIGURE 7.—TUMBLE.

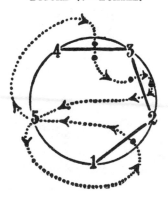

No. 5 raises his left arm, turns outward, moves round to his left outside No. 1 and stands between Nos. 1 and 2, resting his back upon No. 1's sword. He then turns a back somersault over No. 1's rapper and returns backwards to his place.

Raising his right arm, he then moves round to his right, outside No. 4, and stands between Nos. 4 and 3, where he repeats the same performance.

Making a quarter turn clockwise and moving a step to his right, he now stands between Nos. 2 and 3, places his feet together and jumps over No. 2's sword, Nos. 2 and 3 lowering the sword under his feet as he does so.

He then rests his back upon No. 2's sword, turns a back somersault over it and returns to his place.

The Nut is then tied in the usual way.

Figure 8.—Figure Eight.

This is the same figure as Right-And-Left (*see* p. 79).

Figure 9.—Raffally.

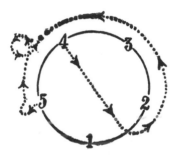

No. 4 moves forward, passes under No. 1's sword, turns to his left and dances round and outside the circle counter-clockwise, passing outside Nos. 2 and 3. Simultaneously, No. 5 raises his right arm, makes a three-quarter revolution on his own axis clockwise, moves a step or two forward, and meets No. 4 face to face. No. 5 now makes a complete revolution on his axis counter-clockwise, and then, followed by No. 4, proceeds to move round in a circle counter-clockwise. When No. 5 has completed three quarters of his first circuit and is facing the audience, No. 1, raising his right arm, turns outward to his right and, followed by Nos. 2 and 3, moves round in a circle clockwise.

The Nut can only be tied when Nos. 1 and 5 are just entering upon a new circuit. Nos. 1, 5 and 4 then stand still; while Nos. 2 and 3 move round counter-clockwise, outside Nos. **1, 5** and 4, pass under No. 4's sword, make each a half turn counter-clockwise and face centre.

Nos. 1 and 5 then move forwards and face centre, each making a half turn, **No. 1** clockwise, and No. 5 counter-clockwise.

This, it will be found, ties the Nut.

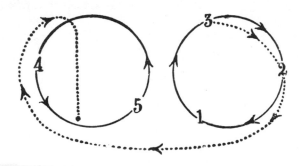

FIGURE 10.—THE PRINCE OF WALES.

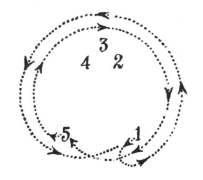

Nos. 2 and 4 close up and stand beside No. 3 in the position shown in the diagram. No. 1 then raises his left arm, turns outward to his left, passes round and outside them, counter-clockwise, and returns to his place; while No. 5 raises his right arm, turns outward to his right passes round and outside the three stationary dancers, clockwise, and resumes his place. No. 1 passes outside No. 5 on first meeting him, and inside when he meets him the second time.

Nos. 1 and 5 now stand close beside No. 3, while Nos. 2 and 4 move round and outside them —No. 2 counter-clockwise, and No. 4 clockwise. No. 2 passes No. 4 first on the outside and then on the inside. No. 3 remains stationary throughout the figure.

The Nut is tied in the usual way directly Nos. 2 and 4 have resumed their places.

FIGURE 11.—DOCTOR COOK.

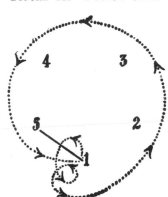

No. 1 leaps over No. 5's sword, raises both arms, revolves once on his axis counter-clockwise, and then, turning to his left, moves outside and round the circle counter-clockwise and returns to his place. Nos. 2, 3, 4 and 5 then do likewise, each in turn jumping over the rapper belonging to the dancer on his left and performing the evolutions above described.

The Nut is tied in the usual way directly No. 5 has resumed his place.

EARSDON SWORD-DANCERS.
THE LEADER HOLDING UP THE NUT.

EARSDON SWORD-DANCE.
FIXY (see p. 97).

Figure 12.—Fixy.

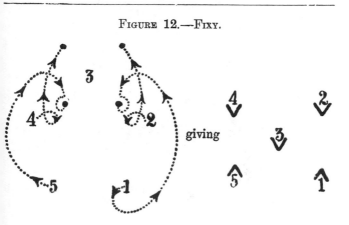

All move round clockwise until No. 3 faces audience.

No. 1, raising his left arm, then turns outward to his left, passes outside No. 2, moves forward between Nos. 2 and 3 (under No. 2's sword), makes a half turn clockwise and stands with his back to the audience on No. 3's left front.

Simultaneously, No. 5, keeping his face to the centre, passes behind No. 4, advances between Nos. 3 and 4 (under No. 3's sword), and, making a half turn counter-clockwise, stands with his back to the audience on No. 3's right front.

No. 2 now makes a one and a quarter turn counter-clockwise, moves backward and stands behind No. 3, facing No. 1; while No. 4 makes a one and a quarter turn clockwise, backs behind No. 3 and faces No. 5 (*see* plate facing p. 97).

The dancers, standing in this position, " step " (eight bars).

The Nut is then tied in the following way. No. 3 moves forward, passes under No. 5's sword, turns to his left and lances round and outside Nos. 1 and 2, halts between Nos. 2 and 4 and faces centre.

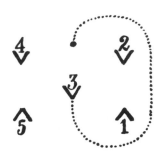

No. 1 then raises his left arm, turns outward and ties the Nut in the usual manner.

FIGURE 13.—THE OLD FIDDLER.

All move round clockwise until No. 3 is facing the audience. The rest also face audience, Nos. 1, 2 and 5 turning counter-clockwise and No. 4 clockwise, and stand thus :—

In this position they step until the end of the strain of the music (eight bars).

No. 5 now turns outwards to his right and moves into No. 3's position ; No. 1 turns outwards to his left and takes No. 2's place ; Nos. 4 and 2 move forwards to the front rank ; and No. 3 takes No. 4's position, thus :—

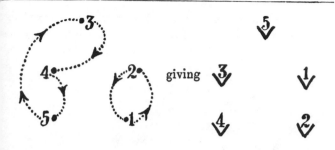

Standing in this position all " step " until the end of the strain (eight bars). Whereupon, a similar change of position is again made, thus :—

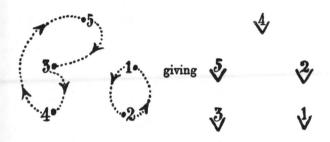

In this position they all " step " as before.

The next change is made a little differently. The front right (No. 1) now goes to the back and No. 3 moves one place back ; while the rest move as before, thus :—

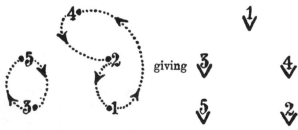

After " stepping " as before, No. 2 moves into the back place;
No. 5 takes No. 3's place, and No. 1 takes No. 4's; while
Nos. 4 and 3 move forwards to the front line, thus :—

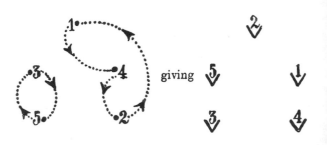

After " stepping " as before, the next and last change is
effected in the following way.   No. 3 moves to the back
place ; No. 2 takes No. 1's place ; Nos. 5 and 1 move into the
two front places ; while No. 4 turns outward to his left,
passes between the second rank and the hindmost, and takes
No. 5's place, thus :—

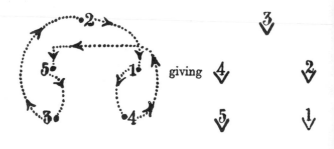

The dancers, once again in their original places, now " step "
until the end of the strain (eight bars).

Immediately the " stepping " is finished, No. 5 makes a
three-quarter turn clockwise, after which the Nut can be
tied in the usual way.

FIGURE 14.—DOCTOR PARRY.

No. 1 jumps over No. 3's sword (Nos. 3 and 4 lowering the sword as he does so, after the manner of a skipping-rope), turns left, and returns to his place. Nos. 2, 3, 4 and 5 then do the same, each, in turn, jumping over the sword belonging to the second dancer on his right and returning, counter-clockwise, to his place.

The Nut is then tied in the usual way.

FIGURE 15.—WAVES.

This is the same as Changy, except that No. 1 always crosses over from one circle to the other *before*, instead of *behind* No. 5.

FIGURE 16.—DOUBLE-GUARD.

This is a variant of The Prince of Wales, in which the two couples pass round simultaneously instead of in succession. Nos. 1 and 2 move round counter-clockwise, and Nos. 4 and 5 clockwise. Upon meeting, Nos. 1 and 2 pass outside the first time, and inside the second time.

The Nut is then tied in the usual way.

FIGURE 17.—FACE-UP.

Nos. 1 and 2 move forward, pass between Nos. 3 and 4 (under No. 3's sword), make each a half turn counter-clockwise, and stand beside No. 3 (No. 2 on No. 1's left) facing audience. No. 5 moves a step backward into line with the others, thus :—

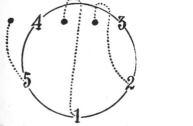 

In this position the dancers " step " (8 bars).

Nos. 1 and 2 now walk forward under No. 3's sword and No. 1 raises both arms, turns to his left, followed by Nos. 2, 3 and 4 and ties the Nut in the ordinary way.

The dancers then form into line and " step," the leader, in the middle, holding up the Nut in his right hand well above his head (8 bars).

This concludes the dance.

NOTATION.

MOVEMENTS.

Introduction (*see* p. 84).
Fig. 1. Single-Guard (*see* p. 90).
Fig. 2. The Nut (*see* p. 90).
Fig. 1. Single-Guard (*see* p. 90).
Fig. 3. Three-and-Two (*see* p. 91).
Figs. 2 and 1. The Nut and Single-Guard.
Fig. 4. Turn-In (*see* p. 92).
Figs. 2 and 1. The Nut and Single-Guard.
Fig. 5. Follow-We (*see* p. 92).
Figs. 2 and 1. The Nut and Single-Guard.
Fig. 6. Changy (*see* p. 92).
Figs. 2 and 1. The Nut and Single-Guard.
Fig. 7. Tumble (*see* p. 93).
Figs. 2 and 1. The Nut and Single-Guard.
Fig. 8. Figure Eight (*see* p. 94).
Figs. 2 and 1. The Nut and Single-Guard.
Fig. 9. Raffally (*see* p. 94).
Figs. 2 and 1. The Nut and Single-Guard.
Fig. 10. The Prince of Wales (*see* p. 95).
Figs. 2 and 1. The Nut and Single-Guard.
Fig. 11. Doctor Cook (*see* p. 96).
Figs. 2 and 1. The Nut and Single-Guard.
Fig. 12. Fixy (*see* p. 97).
Figs. 2 and 1. The Nut and Single-Guard.
Fig. 13. The Old Fiddler (*see* p. 98).

Figs. 2 and 1. The Nut and Single-Guard.
Fig. 14. Doctor Parry (*see* p. 101).
Figs. 2 and 1. The Nut and Single-Guard.
Fig. 15. Waves (*see* p. 101).
Figs. 2 and 1. The Nut and Single-Guard.
Fig. 16. Double-Guard (*see* p. 101).
Figs. 2 and 1. The Nut and Single-Guard.
Fig. 17. Face-Up (*see* p. 101).
Fig. 2. The Nut.
Form up in line and exhibit Nut (*see* p. 102).

THE HORN DANCE, ABBOTS BROMLEY

CHAPTER III

THE
ABBOTS BROMLEY HORN-DANCE.

THERE are ten performers, six dancers, a fool, Maid Marian, a hobby-horse, and a boy carrying a bow and arrow. These are accompanied by a musician, who plays an accordion, and a boy with a triangle.

Each dancer carries a pair of reindeer horns of great size, some of which weigh between 80 and 90 pounds apiece. The antlers borne by the first three dancers are painted a white or cream colour, the remaining three a dark blue. The horns are set in a wooden counterfeit skull, from which depends a short wooden pole or handle about eighteen inches long. Each dancer bears the head in front of him, and supports it by grasping the handle with his right hand and balancing the horns with his left.

The fool has a stick with a bladder attached to it; Maid Marian who, as usual, is impersonated by a man dressed in woman's clothes, carries a wooden ladle which is used to collect money; and the boy holds a bow and arrow which he clicks together in time with the music. The form of the hobby-horse is shown in the accompanying photograph. The head is made of wood, painted, and furnished with a hairy mane. The lower jaw is attached to the upper by a hinge which is worked by a string so that the rider can snap the jaws together in time with the music.

The actual dresses now worn by the performers (*see* photograph) are copies, more or less exact, of some that were devised by a local resident about twenty-five or thirty years ago. As, therefore, there is no traditional authority for them, there is no need to describe them in detail.

THE MUSIC.

There is no special or traditional tune for the dance. The musician told me that any country-dance air would serve, provided that it was played in the proper time (in Common Time $\downarrow = 108$). When I saw the dance performed two tunes only were played, "Yankee Doodle" and the following simple little melody :—

In a letter written in 1893 by the vicar of the parish (*see* "Folk-Lore Journal," vol. iv., p. 172), it is stated that a special tune used to be played for the horn dance by a man with a fiddle, and within the memory of some then living, but that all efforts to recover it had failed.

THE STEP.

The step is very similar to the normal country-dance step. It is an easy, rhythmical, graceful and springy walking movement, executed entirely on the ball of the foot, and in a jaunty manner which is highly characteristic and extremely engaging. The performers hold themselves erect, heads up and backs straight, bear themselves with dignity and preserve a grave demeanour. The steps fall on the first and middle beats of the bar throughout the dance, with one trifling exception presently to be explained.

The dance is performed annually on the Monday in the Wakes week, that is on the day following the first Sunday after the fourth of September. The horns and other properties are in the custody of the Vicar and are kept in the church tower.

There is a tradition that at one time the dance used to be performed on certain Sunday mornings in front of the church porch, and a collection made for the poor. The earliest account of the dance is, probably, that given by Dr. Plot in his " Natural History of Staffordshire " (1686). As this is of great interest it will bear quotation in full :—

" At Abbots, or now rather Pagets Bromley, they had also, within memory, a sort of sport, which they celebrated at

Christmas (on New-year and Twelft-day) call'd the Hobby-horse dance, from a person that carryed the image of a horse between his legs, made of thin boards, and in his hand a bow and arrow, which passing through a hole in the bow, and stopping upon a sholder it had in it, he made a snapping noise as he drew it to and fro, keeping time with the Music: with this man danced six others, carrying on their shoulders as many Rain deers heads, 3 of them painted white, and 3 red, with the Armes of the cheif families (viz. of Paget, Bagot, and Wells) to whom the revenews of the Town cheifly belonged, depicted on the palms of them, with which they danced the Hays, and other Country dances. To this Hobby-horse dance there also belong'd a pot, which was kept by turnes, by 4 or 5 of the cheif of the Town, whom they call'd Reeves, who provided Cakes and Ale to put in this pot; all people who had any kindness for the good intent of the Institution of the sport, giving pence a piece for themselves and families; and so forraigners too, that came to see it: with which Mony (the charge of the Cakes and Ale being defrayed) they not only repaired their Church but kept their poore too: which charges are not now perhaps so cheerfully boarn."

Interesting as this account is, the words "within memory," implying that Dr. Plot wrote from his own or others' recollections, and these of no very recent date, render inference as to subsequent changes in the custom, based on omissions and differences of detail in his description, somewhat precarious.

On the one hand, however, it will be noticed that the dance was performed at Christmas time; that the bow was carried by the rider of the hobby-horse; that the horns were borne on the shoulders instead of in the hands of the dancers; and that no mention is made either of a fool or of Maid Marian.

On the other hand we find that the bearer of the bow and arrow still makes the snapping noise "keeping time with the Music"; that the number of the dancers is the same; and that the dance itself has changed very little. For the Hays evidently refers to the serpentine movement which is the chief and the most characteristic feature of the modern dance; while the second evolution, " All-Together," is, of course, a well known country-dance figure.   It is greatly to be regretted that Dr. Plot made no reference to the music nor to the costumes worn by the dancers.

Other accounts of the dance will be found in P. H. Ditchfield's "Old English Customs," p. 139, and in "The Folk-Lore Journal," vol. iv., p. 172, and vol. vii., p. 382.

THE DANCE.

The performers stand in single file, one behind the other, headed by the leader, and in the following order :—

> 1.
> 2.
> 3.
> 4. } Dancers carrying horns.
> 5.
> 6.
> 7. Maid Marian.
> 8. Hobby-horse.
> 9. Boy with bow and arrow.
> 10. The Fool.

Led by No. 1, they first move forward a few yards in a straight line and then describe a circular or elliptic track in either direction, say, clockwise.   If space permits, the circle should be large enough to allow of a clear space of at least ten yards between the head and tail of the procession.

After completing one or more revolutions, the leader suddenly turns inwards, and faces No. 2.   Poising himself for a moment, while taking two or three short steps backward, he then passes between Nos. 3 and 4, turns sharply to his left, dances close to and outside the rest of the dancers, and initiates a new circular movement in the reverse direction, counter-clockwise.

Immediately No. 1 faces No. 2, No. 4, followed by those behind him, moves inwards to his right along the track shown in the diagram, shaping his course and regulating his pace so that he falls in naturally behind No. 3:—

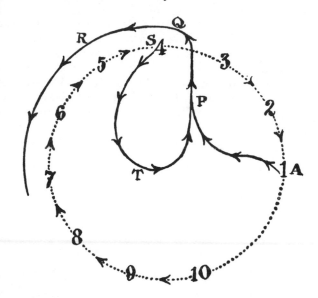

The dotted line in the above diagram shows the original track. A is the point where the leader doubles back and faces No. 2; and A P Q R the course along which he then proceeds, followed, as far as P, by Nos. 2 and 3 and, subsequently, by the rest of the procession.

No. 4, with those behind him, moves along the line S T P Q R joining No. 1's track at P at the moment when No. 3 has just passed by. The success of the evolution very largely depends upon the skill with which No. 4 shapes his course and orders his pace.

These circular and serpentine movements are repeated, in alternation, as often as the leader elects. He then calls " All-Together," turns sharply to his left (*i.e.*, if he is going round clockwise; otherwise, to his right) and, followed by Nos. 2 and 3, proceeds in a straight line across the circle, as shown in the diagram.   Simultaneously, Nos. 4, 5, 6, 7 and 8 edge towards the left until they are in a straight line parallel to and about five yards away from the path described by the leader.   When the latter is opposite to No. 6, all, except Nos. 9 and 10, halt and make a quarter turn inwards, so that Nos. 1, 2 and 3 face one way and Nos. 4, 5, 6, 7 and 8 in the opposite direction.

Immediately No. 1 initiates this movement, Nos. 10 and 9 make a half turn to their left and, bearing to the right, dance towards and meet No. 1 ; whereupon they both turn inwards and face, respectively, Nos. 7 and 8.

The dancers are now in two parallel lines facing each other, as shown in the following diagram :—

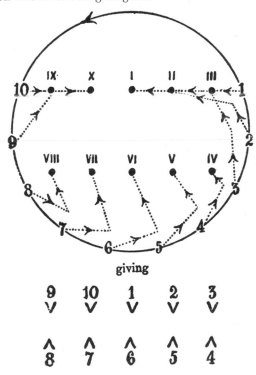

giving

9	10	1	2	3
V	V	V	V	V

∧	∧	∧	∧	∧
8	7	6	5	4

Standing in this position the two lines of dancers wait until the beginning of the next strain of the music. They then move forward and meet; each dancer beginning with his left foot, taking three steps forward and then, instead of a fourth step, throwing his right leg forward, while he swings both hands forward and upward (two bars).

They then take four steps backward to their places, beginning with right feet (two bars).

These forward and backward movements are then repeated twice (eight bars).

The two lines of dancers now cross over and change sides, partners passing left shoulder to left shoulder, turning inwards and facing each other (four bars).

All the above movements are then repeated in the reverse direction; and this brings the dancers back to their original positions (sixteen bars, *i.e.*, thirty-two bars in all).

This concludes the figure, which is repeated or not at the leader's discretion. On its conclusion the dancers form up in single file and begin the dance over again.

To form line the leader faces outward, turns sharply to his right, followed by Nos. 2 and 3; No. 4, followed by Nos. 5, 6 7 and 8, falls in behind No. 3; while No. 9, with No. 10 behind him, follows No. 8.

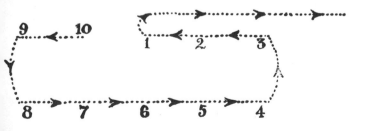

The above movements are executed whenever the dancers perform in a stationary position before a special audience. When, however, they are proceeding from one "stand" to another they dance in the way shown in the following diagram :—

The unbroken line shows the track taken by Nos. 1, 2, and 3 ; whenever No. 4, with those behind him, follows a different course the latter is indicated by a dotted line.

FLAMBOROUGH SWORD DANCERS (JUNIOR TEAM).

THE LOCK (see p. 37).

THE

SWORD-DANCES

OF

NORTHERN ENGLAND

COLLECTED AND DESCRIBED

BY

CECIL J. SHARP.

PART II.

PREFACE.

THE thanks of the Author are due to the dancers whose performances are described in this book, especially to Mr. Richard Major and Mr. William Major of Flamborough, to Mr. G. Hall of Beadnell, and to Mr. Benjamin Breckon and Mr. J. Smithies of Eskdaleside, Sleights.

The Author desires also to acknowledge the help that he has received in his investigations from Mrs. Ward, Mrs. Baines, the Revd. E. M. Adamson, Mr. Parker Brewis and Mr. E. Isle Hubbard ; and to express his gratitude to Mr. E. Phillips Barker for reading and criticising the proofs.

CONTENTS.

INTRODUCTION.

The two Yorkshire dances, from Flamborough and Sleights, belong, like all that have so far been found in that county, to the long-sword species and must be classed, therefore, with the Grenoside and Kirkby Malzeard dances described in Part I. Each dance has, however, an individuality of its own, and characteristics which differentiate it from other long-sword dances. Variety, indeed, appears to be one of the chief attributes of this type of dance, a quality which makes it peculiarly acceptable to performers and, incidentally, of more than ordinary interest to the collector.

In the Flamborough dance, for instance, the number of the performers is unusual, viz., eight; wooden swords are used instead of metal ones; the figures and movements are new, with the possible exception of the reversing ring movements (Single-threedling), which bear some resemblance to the opening figure of the Abbots Bromley Horn-dance (*see* Part I, pp. 108-9). In construction, too, the Flamborough dance is different from other Yorkshire dances, although, in the concluding figures with unlinked swords, which form an appendix to the dance—the casting-off, weaving, and hey—we are reminded of " The Reel and Roll " and " Jolly Lads " of the Grenoside and Kirkby dances. Again, emotionally, it strikes a new note. It is an extremely spirited and vivacious dance; indeed, the performers must be in first-rate physical condition to go through with it properly and effectively. On the whole, the Flamborough dance may be regarded, I think, artistically and from a spectacular point of view, as one of the best of the Yorkshire sword-dances.

Apart from its æsthetic qualities as a dance, and they are many, the Sleights sword-dance will make a special appeal to the folk-lorist as well as to the analyst and student of folk-dance; to the former because of the quaint ceremonial observances which accompany the annual performance on Plough Monday; and to the latter in that it supplies a link between the long-sword dances of Yorkshire and the rapper-dances of Northumberland. It has a structure the same as that of the typical rapper-dance, being divided into figures, each of which begins with the same ritual and ends with the tying and exhibition of the Nut, with a distinctive movement interposed between them. Again, in Double-Under, the distinctive movement of the third Figure, a faint suggestion of the typical bi-circle movement of the rapper-dance is to be detected. These two points of similarity are very significant and of no small interest; for, hitherto, it has been difficult to trace, technically, any connection between the stiff-sword and flexible-sword dances. Remembering the geographical position of Sleights, in the extreme north-east corner of Yorkshire, we may hope that in some of the villages between the Esk and the Tyne sword-dances still exist which will furnish yet more links in the chain connecting these two dissimilar species of dance. In the meanwhile the Sleights dance is valuable for its suggestion of a possible solution of a very puzzling problem.

Two other movements in the dance call for comment. The three new methods of tying the Lock are especially noteworthy, and afford a pleasing relief to the two ways in which this operation has always hitherto been performed; one of them, the Back-Lock, is particularly ingenious.

The movement called " Elbows " in the text reminds us of the wide distribution of the sword-dance. In the "Folk-Lore Journal" (vol. v., pp. 312-14), a description is given of the " Bacchu-Ber, a Pyrrhic Dance of the High Alps," translated from the French (1820), the sixth figure of which is thus described:—"Each makes one step to the left on his heel; then, still holding his own sword and his neighbour's also, makes a movement with his arms so as to bring his *right* wrist beneath his *left* elbow, and his left wrist in front of his hip, and thus they execute a *pas de deux* towards the left."

A reference to the picture facing page 19 will show that this is an accurate description of the position shown in the photograph.

The following description of the dance as it was performed nearly a century ago is not without value, because it shows how very little, in matters essential, it has altered during that period:—

" On Plough Monday, the first Monday after Twelfth Day, and some days following, there is a procession of rustic youths dragging a plough, who, as they officiate for *oxen*, are called *plough-stots*. They are dressed with their shirts on the outside of their jackets, with sashes of ribbons fixed across their breasts and backs, and knots or roses of ribbons fastened on the shirts and on their hats. Besides the plough-draggers, there is a band of six, in the same dress, furnished with swords, who perform the sword-dance, while one or more musicians play on the fiddle or flute. The sword-dance, probably introduced by the Danes, displays considerable ingenuity, not without gracefulness. The dancers arrange themselves in a ring with their swords elevated; and their motions and evolutions are at first slow and simple, but become gradually more rapid and complicated: towards the close, each one catches the point of his neighbour's sword, and various movements take place in consequence, one of which consists in joining or plaiting the swords into the form of an elegant hexagon or rose in the centre of the ring, which rose is so firmly made, that one of them holds it up above their heads without undoing it. The dance closes with taking it to pieces, each man laying hold of his own sword. During the dance, two or three of the company, called *Toms* or *clowns*, dressed up as harlequins in the most fantastic modes, having their faces painted or masked, are making antic gestures and movements to amuse the spectators; while another set, called *Madgies*, or *Madgy-Pegs*, clumsily dressed in women's clothes, and also masked or painted, go about from door to door, rattling old canisters in which they receive money. When they are well paid they raise a huzza; where they get nothing they shout 'Hunger and starvation!' When the party do not exceed forty they seldom encumber themselves with a plough. They parade from town to town for two or three days, and the money collected is then expended in a feast and dance, to which the girls who furnished the ribbons and other decorations are invited. Sometimes the sword-dance is performed differently; a kind of farce, in which songs are introduced, being acted along with the dance. The principal characters in the farce are the *king*, the *miller*, the *clown*, and the *doctor*.

"Egton Bridge has long been the chief rendezvous for sword-dancers in this vicinity" ("A History of Whitby and Streoneshalh Abbey," by the Rev. George Young, 1817, pp. 880-1).

The Plough Monday ceremony is, of course, closely associated with the agricultural seasonal festivals to which, in the Introduction of Part I, an attempt was made to trace the origin of the sword-dance. Mr. Chambers thinks it probably "represents an early spring perambulation of the fields in which the divinity rode upon a plough" ("The Mediæval Stage," i., p. 299).

The Plough Stots were sometimes called the Fond Plows or Fool Plows. Under the former designation they performed, within living memory, in the neighbourhood of Flamborough, and under the latter in the district around Ely. Originally a religious observance, the festival in later days came to serve the more prosaic function of enforcing a resumption of farming operations, relaxed during the preceding "twelve days of Christmas," *i.e.*, the customary holiday between Christmas and the Epiphany.

The Beadnell rapper-dance is a variant, and a fairly close one, of the Swalwell dance. It contains, however, certain movements which are new, *e.g.*, the ring position with backs to the centre, which follows the Rose; the distinctive movements of the fourth and fifth Figures; and the postponement of the exhibition of the Nut to the close of the dance.

DRAGONFIELD, UXBRIDGE,
     March, 1912.

SLEIGHTS SWORD DANCERS.
THE LOCK (*see p.* 20).

THE SLEIGHTS SWORD-DANCE.

SLEIGHTS is a small agricultural village in the North Riding of Yorkshire, about three miles inland from Whitby.

The Sleights Plough Stots, or Eskdaleside Sword Dancers as they are sometimes called, perform annually on Plough Monday, the first Monday after Twelfth Day, and the following days. This year the party numbered fourteen —six dancers, seven " Toms," and a fiddler. Formerly, the dancers were accompanied by a band of youths dragging a plough, decked with ribbons and greenery—hence the term " Plough Stot," *i.e.*, plough bullock. This custom has long been discontinued.

The dancers wear red soldier-tunics with white collars, and white stuff or silk sashes round their waists, about two-and-a-half to three inches wide, fastened in a bow at the back or at the side, or worn like a belt ; black trousers, and ordinary cloth caps. Each dancer carries a sword with a bunch of ribbons attached to the hilt. The blade is of steel, about twenty-eight inches long and one inch in width, and has a rib down the middle ; at the tip, instead of a point, there is a metal circle, about the size of a shilling, with a hole in the centre for the attachment of ribbons. The hilt, on the top of which ribbons of various colours are nailed, is round, and made of wood.

The Toms (*see* Plate facing pp. 19 and 20) wear loose tunics of bright patterned stuff with a woollen fringe round the lower edge and round the yoke, covered with tags of lace, bunches of ribbons, rosettes, feathers, and patches of coloured cloth or

B

silk, cut into various shapes, *e.g.*, birds and animals of all kinds, squares, stars, circles, diamonds, etc. In one instance the picture of a plough and horses, cut out in cloth, was stitched on to the back of the coat, across the shoulders. The trousers are made of motley cotton stuff, ornamented like the tunics. The hats, of felt or straw, are very large and completely hidden beneath a pile of artificial flowers, ribbons, coloured crimped paper, and feathers. All black their faces, wholly or in part, and wear beards made of white, black, or red wool. They told me that they blacked their faces and wore beards so that "no one might know them." Each Tommy carries a sword and a tin collecting box, and his main business is to solicit money from any and everyone. On their way from Sleights to Whitby they stopped every cart, carriage, motor-car, bicycle, etc., they met, solicited labourers in the fields, masons and bricklayers on buildings, and knocked at the door of every cottage and house they passed on the road. Sometimes, when the doors were barred and they were refused admittance, they would climb in through the windows. Their persistence was received good-humouredly enough, in the same spirit in which it was offered ; and it was clear that their importunities were regarded by everyone as a legitimate and essential part of the ceremony. In the old days when they had the plough with them, if a householder or farmer refused to contribute, they would punish his churlishness by ploughing a furrow through his lawn or his best pasture.

The festivities used to be continued day by day throughout the week. This year they were, however, content with two days, the first of which they spent in their own village and Whitby, and the second at Robin Hood's Bay. On the evening of the last day a meeting is held, the money counted up, and after expenses are deducted, apportioned amongst the several members of the party. Each man contributes two shillings from his share to pay for the supper and dance that is held on the following Saturday night, to which, if he pleases, he may bring his sweetheart. In order to incite the Toms to do their best, a small prize is awarded to him who collects the most money.

I accompanied the dancers throughout the greater part of Plough Monday, and I can testify to the light-hearted, cheery, holiday spirit which animated everyone. It is true that passers-by were mercilessly chaffed and rallied with good-humoured persistence until they paid up; but I saw no horse-play or vulgarity of any kind.

From Mr. Benjamin Breckon, of Eskdaleside, an old dancer, I gathered the following information. There used to be, so he told me, teams of Plough Stots at Aislaby, Goathland, Robin Hood's Bay, and Egton Bridge, but none of these are now in existence. He could not remember any Captain, Fool, or Betty, but the dancers used to be accompanied by a Tom, whom they called the Clown, and who would go into the ring in the last figure and have the locked swords placed round his throat. As recently as fifteen or twenty years ago, they were also accompanied by a King, wearing a black frock-coat and a box hat, and a Queen, a man dressed in woman's garb, with long black ringlets of hair hanging down his back and a thick veil over his face. These two characters were taken seriously, and behaved in a dignified way and kept order. They usually walked arm-in-arm at the head of the dancers as they marched from place to place.

Mr. Breckon also told me that, in his father's time, the party numbered as many as a hundred. There were two teams of dancers, a large number of Toms, and a plough drawn by horses. A man dressed like a policeman went with them to keep order; and the procession was headed by three men wearing long cloaks, "like gentlemen," riding on grey horses. They often received a warm reception in Whitby, especially from the fisherwomen, who would pelt them from the windows with mud, eggs, &c., and sometimes red-hot coppers. " Going a-Tomming " in those days must have been a perilous and exciting adventure.

Of the two teams of dancers one wore red coats with blue facings, the other blue coats with red facings; both wore a white sash round the waist, black trousers with red stripes down the legs, and caps trimmed with a coloured riband hanging down over one ear. Two ribbons, red and blue, were fastened to the tip of each sword. Red and blue, Mr. Breckon explained, were in those days the colours of the two political parties; so that when they performed before an important house, they were able to present a team dressed in accordance with the political colour of the resident.

The Toms had picture-ploughs on their backs, with the legend " God speed the plough "; bands of straw or hay round their knees; turkey feathers, pieces of fox's skin—an old duck's head was greatly prized—in their hats, with a ring of wheat-ears round the brim. Sometimes they would wear large wooden spectacles, so that " no one would know them." Fourteen Tommies was the usual number. When soliciting contributions, they would cry, " Remember the plough," " Shake a bawbee," or " Sing a bawbee."

Besides the recognised team of sword-dancers, there is at Sleights a team of youths who imitate their elders and perambulate the village later in the week. In this way boys are trained in the dance, so that when they are grown up they are ready to be drafted into the senior team as the older men drop out.

THE MUSIC.

Of the five parts of this dance, "No Man's Jig " is invariably danced to the tune given in the Music Book*; the other four possess no airs traditionally associated with them, but each is usually danced to a different tune. At the performances this year the fiddler played the following

---

* "The Sword-Dances of England: Songs and Dance-Airs," Book II.

SLEIGHTS SWORD DANCERS.
THE CLASH (*see p.* 19).

airs: "Bobby Shaftoe," "Old Mother Hi Ti," "Pop goes the Weasel," "The Girl I left behind me," and "Cock o' the North." The first of these I have called "Bobbie Shaftoe," because it was so named by the fiddler and the dancers, but it is quite different from the air usually associated with that song (*see* "Northumbrian Minstrelsy," p. 115). "Old Mother Hi Ti" was but another name for "The Rakes of Mallow."

As in other sword-dances, the music controls the step throughout, but the evolutions also are to some extent under its control. Thus in each of the first four Figures, for the Clash and Shoulders-and-Elbows the whole tune is played through twice; for Your-Neighbour's-Sword, Double-Over, Double-Under, or Double-Under-and-Double-Over, together with the making of the Lock, the tune is played as many times as the evolution requires. In whichever strain of the music the Lock happens to be made, the musician must be careful to follow on with the *first* strain. The display of the Lock will then occupy the first strain of the final repeat, and the performance of the Rose the second. In "No Man's Jig," as will be seen, both steps and movements are strictly controlled throughout.

THE STEP.

Throughout the dance the performers take two steps to each bar of the music (except in the first movement of "No Man's Jig," where *four* steps are taken in the bar). In quality, the step is a decided march or tramp; so at least it was when the team were on the road, but when they were rehearsing in their practising room I noticed that they moved with greater energy, springing from foot to foot like soldiers at the double. It may be that this is the proper and traditional step which, for obvious reasons, they modified when they had to dance at frequent intervals during a tramp of several hours, often on rough ground.

THE DANCE.

The six dancers stand in a ring, facing centre, resting the points of their swords on the ground, in the following order:

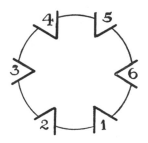

Standing thus, they sing the following song, accompanied by the fiddler :—

> Here's fourteen of us all ;
> From Sleights Town we come,
> And we are going a-ramble-ing
> The country for to see.
>
> And a holiday we will take,
> Some pastime for to make ;
> So freely you will give to us,
> So freely we will take.
>
> Although we are but young
> And never danced here before,
> O we will do the best we can,
> And the best can do no more.
>
> So now you see us all
> Dressed in our bright array,
> Now we will start our dancing,
> So Music strike up and play.

The dance then begins without pause.

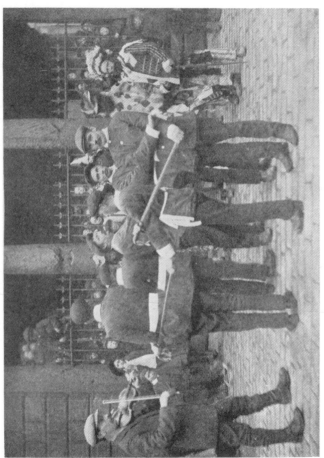

SLEIGHTS SWORD DANCERS.
ELBOWS (*see p. 19*).

FIGURE 1.

THE CLASH.

The dancers move slowly round in a ring, clockwise, raise their swords, points up, towards the centre of the circle (*see* plate facing p. 16) and clash them together on the first and middle beats of each bar of the music, as in the "Kirkby Malzeard Sword Dance" (*see* Part I, p. 44). This is continued for eight bars.

SHOULDERS-AND-ELBOWS.

The dancers now place their swords over their right shoulders and, grasping the points of the swords in front of them with their left hands, march round clockwise (8 bars).

On the first beat of the next strain of the music, they lift their swords over their heads, shift them from right to left shoulders, and march round clockwise as before (8 bars).

On the first beat of the succeeding strain they lower their swords, resting them on their left arms, just above the elbows (*see* plate facing p. 19), and in this position march round clockwise (8 bars).

YOUR NEIGHBOUR'S SWORD.

All raise and pass their swords over their heads, make a quarter-turn clockwise, face centre and stand still, in hilt-and-point position. The Leader, No. 1 (assisted by No. 6, who moves slightly towards him, raising his left arm), then raises his right hand high above his head and jumps over his left neighbour's sword (*i.e.*, No. 2's), making a whole-turn counter-clockwise. No. 2 (similarly assisted by No. 1) then jumps over No. 3's sword in like manner. This movement is then repeated, in turn, by Nos. 3, 4, 5 and 6.

THE RIGHT-AND-LEFT LOCK.

All face centre and, moving slowly round clockwise, cross hands, right over left, and lock the swords in the same way as in the " Kirkby Malzeard Dance " (*see* Part I, page 52).

The dancers continue to move slowly round, clockwise, until the end of the strain of the music. At the beginning of the next strain the Leader, holding the hilt of his own sword in his right hand, raises the Lock high above his head (*see* plate facing p. 13), arm erect, and marches round, clockwise, followed by the rest of the dancers (8 bars).

THE ROSE.

The Leader now lowers the Lock to a horizontal position over the centre of the circle, hip level. Each dancer holds the hilt of his own sword in his right hand and all move round clockwise (8 bars).

On the first beat of the eighth bar the Lock is lifted up about twelve inches and then, on the middle beat of the same bar, suddenly lowered, all simultaneously drawing their swords from the Lock with the greatest vigour.

This concludes the Figure, between which and the next a slight pause is made.

FIGURE 2.

This, like the preceding Figure, begins with the two movements, " The Clash " and " Shoulders-and-Elbows."

DOUBLE-OVER.

This is performed in very much the same way as " Double-Over " in the " Kirkby Malzeard Dance " (*see* Part I, p. 49), except that, (1) the order is varied, Nos. 3 and 4, 4 and 5, 5 and 6, 6 and 1, 1 and 2, and 2 and 3 successively holding down the sword between them ; and (2) the two dancers who lower the sword jump over it simultaneously, and turn in to their places directly after the second couple has passed over.

THE NIP-IT LOCK.

All face centre, raise both hands well above their heads, make a whole turn clockwise, lower their arms (crossed left over right) and close in. Slowly moving round clockwise they tie the swords together, each man thrusting his hilt under the nearest point on his left. They continue moving round until the end of the strain of the music.

At the beginning of the next strain the Leader raises the Lock, as in the preceding Figure, and all march round clockwise (8 bars).

The Rose is then performed in the way described in the last Figure. A slight pause is made between this and the succeeding Figure.

FIGURE 3.

This, like the two preceding Figures, begins with " The Clash " and " Shoulders-and-Elbows."

DOUBLE-UNDER.

This is very similar to " Double Under" in the " Kirkby Malzeard Sword Dance " (*see* Part I, p. 49). The order, however, is the same as that of "Double-Over " in the preceding Figure ; that is to say, Nos. 3 and 4 make the first arch, followed, in turn, by Nos. 4 and 5, 5 and 6, 6 and 1, 1 and 2, and 2 and 3. The method is, too, a little different. In the first change, for instance, Nos. 3 and 4, while

Nos. 1 and 6 and Nos. 2 and 5 are passing through the arch, move slowly inward towards the centre, make a half-turn (No. 3 counter-clockwise, and No. 4 clockwise), and face Nos. 1 and 6. Nos. 1 and 6, directly they have passed through the arch, make a half-turn (No. 1 counter-clockwise, No. 6 clockwise), and face Nos. 3 and 4.

These two couples now move towards each other; Nos. 3 and 4 pass under No. 1's sword, make a half-turn under their sword (No. 3 counter-clockwise, and No. 4 clockwise) and face centre.

THE BACK LOCK.

All face centre, close in, leave go of the points of the swords in their left hands, pass left arms behind the backs of their left neighbours, and grasp the sword-points belonging to the men two places to their left. At a signal from the Leader all raise their arms over their heads, lower them towards the centre, waist level, and make the Lock, each man placing the hilt of his own sword under the sword-point which he holds in his left-hand. They then move round slowly till the end of the strain of the music.

At the beginning of the next strain, the Leader raises the Lock and all move round clockwise (8 bars).

Then follows the Rose as already described in preceding Figures.

A short pause is made between this and the next Figure.

SLEIGHTS SWORD DANCERS.
THE HIGH LOCK (*see p.* 23).

FIGURE 4.

As in the preceding Figures, this begins with " The Clash " and " Shoulders-and-Elbows."

Double-Under and Double-Over.

This Figure consists of six movements, alternately Double-Under and Double-Over, in the following order:—

Double-Under, Nos. 3 and 4 holding up the sword between them.

Double-Over, Nos. 6 and 1 holding down the sword between them.

Double-Under, Nos. 5 and 6 holding up the sword between them.

Double-Over, Nos. 2 and 3 holding down the sword between them.

Double-Under, Nos. 1 and 2 holding up the sword between them.

Double-Over, Nos. 4 and 5 holding down the sword between them.

It will be seen that the arch-couple in Double-Under is the first couple to pass over the swords in the succeeding Double-Over.

The High Lock.

All face centre, close in, raise arms above their heads, and make a half-turn, clockwise. Moving slowly round, clockwise, in this position, backs to the centre, arms erect, wrists crossed (left under right), they lock the swords together, each man separating his hands and placing his hilt under the nearest sword-point. They then make a half-turn, clockwise, face centre, release left hands and, keeping the Lock raised by supporting it with right hands, move round slowly,

c

clockwise, until the end of the strain of the music. At
the beginning of the next strain, the Leader raises the Lock
in the way described in previous Figures and all move round,
clockwise (8 bars).

The Rose follows as before. A short pause is made
between this and the final Figure, " No Man's Jig."

NO MAN'S JIG.

Two of the Toms, armed with swords, now join the dancers,
making eight in all. The dancers stand in two files of four,
facing front as in a " Longways Country Dance." The
two Toms stand at the top. For convenience' sake the
dancers will now be re-numbered, thus :—

	2.	4.	6.	8.	
Top.	V	V	V	V	Bottom.
	∧	∧	∧	∧	
	1.	3.	5.	7.	

Music　　　　　　　CHANGE-AND-CLASH.
A1.

Bar 1.　　　Nos. 3, 4, 7 and 8 cast off (*i.e.*, turn outwards,
　　　　　　　Nos. 3 and 7 to their right, Nos. 4 and 8 to
　　　　　　　their left) and move up one place ; while
　　　　　　　Nos. 1, 2, 5 and 6 move down one place. All
　　　　　　　take four steps, one to each crotchet.

„ 2.　　　Nos. 1, 2, 5 and 6 cast off and move up one
　　　　　　　place ; while Nos. 3, 4, 7 and 8 move down
　　　　　　　one place. All are now in their original
　　　　　　　places

Bar 3-4.   All stand in position, facing front. Partners clash their swords together, moving them from right to left, on the middle beat of the fourth bar.

,,   5-6.   Same as in bars 1-2.

,,   7-8.   All stand in position, facing front. Partners clash their swords together three times, on the first and third beats of the seventh bar, and on the first beat of the eighth bar.

A2.   Same as A1.

B1.

Bar 1.   Same as bar 1, A1.

,,   2.   All stand in position, facing front. Partners clash their swords on the middle beat of the bar.

,,   3.   Same as bar 2, A1.

,,   4.   All stand in position, facing front. Partners clash swords on third beat of the bar.

,,   5-6.   Same as bars 1 and 2, A1.

,,   7-8.   Position, facing front. Partners clash swords on first and third beats of seventh bar and on the first beat of the eighth bar.

B2.   Same as B1.

Partners after clashing, should keep their swords crossed as long as possible.

THE ROLL.

Partners face one another, each taking hold of his partner's sword-point with his left-hand. Partners are thus linked together by two parallel swords in the way described in the "Grenoside Sword Dance" (*see* Part I, p. 64).

The first couple changes places with the second couple, Nos. 3 and 4 moving up one place between Nos. 1 and 2, and under their swords (2 bars, *i.e.*, 4 steps). This is a progressive movement, and is continued after the manner of a progressive country dance (duple minor-set), the dancers going down always passing outside and over those going up.

Throughout this movement the dancers "spin" as they move, *i.e.*, each dancer makes a whole turn on his axis in four steps, as he moves from one place to the next. In going down, odd numbers spin clockwise, even numbers counter-clockwise ; in going up, odd numbers spin counter-clockwise, even numbers clockwise. Neutral couples, while they wait, spin once in the opposite direction from that in which they have previously been turning.

This movement is continued until the Leader determines it. All, including the two Toms (one only, if there is no Queen), then form a ring, facing centre, in hilt-and-point formation, and do the Back Lock (*see* p. 22), afterwards moving round clockwise until the end of the strain of the music. The Leader then raises the Lock in the usual way, and all dance round clockwise (8 bars).

The Queen (or, in her absence, the second Tom) now enters the ring, and the Leader places the Lock over his head and on to his shoulders. Standing thus, with the Lock round his neck, the Queen (or the Tom) moves slowly round counter-clockwise, while the eight (or seven) dancers, each holding his own sword by the hilt, dance round clockwise and perform the Rose. In the final bar the dancers draw their swords from round the Queen's neck in the way previously described.

This concludes the dance.

NOTATION.

INTRODUCTORY SONG.

Fig. 1.   The Clash (*see* p. 19).
Shoulders-and-Elbows (*see* p. 19).
Your-Neighbour's-Sword (*see* p. 19).
Right-and-Left Lock (*see* p. 20).
The Rose (*see* p. 20).

Fig. 2.   The Clash.
Shoulders-and-Elbows.
Double-Over (*see* p. 20).
Nip-It Lock (*see* p. 21).
The Rose.

Fig. 3.   The Clash.
Shoulders-and-Elbows.
Double-Under (*see* p. 21).
The Back Lock (*see* p. 22).
The Rose.

Fig. 4.   The Clash.
Shoulders-and-Elbows.
Double-Under and Double-Over.
The High Lock (*see* p. 23).
The Rose.

No Man's Jig.   Change-and-Clash (*see* p. 24)
The Roll (*see* p. 25).
The Back Lock (*see* p. 22).
The Rose (*see* p. 26).

THE FLAMBOROUGH SWORD-DANCE.

FLAMBOROUGH is a small fishing village about two miles due east of Flamborough Head in the North Riding of Yorkshire. A sword dance is annually performed there a few days before and after Christmas. Occasionally in the summer holidays the dancers perform on the sands at Filey ; but Christmas is regarded as the proper season.

The performers, eight in number, are fishermen. They wear dark blue jerseys, cloth caps of the same colour, white ducks, and black shoes. At one time they used to blacken their faces and wear red jackets decked with rosettes and bunches of gaily coloured ribbons.

Each dancer carries a wooden sword, made of ash or larch, thirty-seven inches long by one-and-a-half wide, shaped at one end into a handle and tapering slightly towards the tip. Nowadays the Leader uses a wooden sword like the rest of the dancers ; but till a few years ago he had a metal one, by the hilt of which he raised the Lock in the course of the dance. I could not find that the dance was ever known as a Morris dance.

I was told that about sixty years ago the dance was revived— by the father of my informant—after it had lapsed for a few seasons. Since then it has, apparently, been performed every Christmas, without break.

I could find no trace of a Captain, Fool, or Betty. The performers, however, are accompanied on their rounds by two men called " beggars," who are dressed like the dancers and carry collecting-boxes and swords similar to those used in the dance. These swords are used to rap on the doors of prospective contributors, and serve also as spare weapons with which to replace the breakages that are apt to occur in the course of the dance

Nor, although I made careful inquiry, could I discover that any acting or singing had ever formed an integral part of the Flamborough Dance. I was told, however, that the dancers regard "Old John Walker," to the tune of which they often dance, as their own special song. This may possibly indicate that at one time, like other sword dances, the Flamborough Dance had its own prefatory song.

From the description that follows it will be seen that no one is enclosed within the meshed swords in either of the "Lock" figures of the dance. One of the dancers told me, however, that in the old days the men would sometimes chase and catch an outsider, *i.e.*, a stranger to the village, and hold him within their locked swords until he paid a ransom.

As at Sleights, there is a junior team of sword dancers at Flamborough (*see* frontispiece), who go out at the same time as their elders.

THE MUSIC.

No special tune is traditionally associated with this dance, "Old John Walker" is perhaps the air which the dancers at the present time most frequently use. But any lively dance tune of two 8-bar strains will serve the purpose so long as it can be effectively played at the requisite speed (M.M. $\downarrow$ or $\downarrow$. = 104).

Two airs, suitable for the purpose, are given in the Music Book, "Three Jolly Sheepskins" and "The Staffordshire Hornpipe."

In Figures 1, 3, 4, 5, 9 and 10 the music, as in the Kirkby Malzeard Sword Dance, controls the steps only. In the remaining Figures the movements synchronise with the music as indicated in the directions.

THE STEP.

Throughout the dance the performers use the " skipping-step " (*see* " Country Dance Book," Part 2, p. 29), *i.e.*, a step-and-hop on alternate feet, thus :—

$$\frac{2}{2} \quad \text{\musicglyph{r.} \quad h.r. \quad l. \quad h.l.} \quad \text{or} \quad \frac{6}{8} \quad \text{r. \quad h.r. \quad l. \quad h.l.}$$

The free leg is not straightened and thrown forward as in the Morris-step.

The skipping-step is executed very vigorously throughout the dance, and continuously, the performers marking-time with the same step even when they are in a stationary position.

THE DANCE.

All through the dance the performers hold their swords in their *left* hands.

FIGURE 1.—RING-AND-LOCK.

The eight dancers form a ring, one behind the other, facing clockwise, in the following order :—

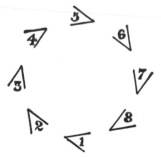

Each man, holding the hilt of his own sword in his left hand, rests it upon his own left shoulder, and grasps the tip of the sword belonging to the man in front of him with his right hand (*see* plate facing p. 30).

FLAMBOROUGH SWORD DANCERS.
RING-AND-LOCK (*see p.* 30).

FLAMBOROUGH SWORD DANCERS (JUNIOR TEAM).
SINGLE-THREEDLING (*c*) (*see p.* 33).

In this formation they dance round, clockwise, with great vigour, until, at a signal from the Leader, all suddenly stop. They lift their swords over their heads, make a quarter-turn clockwise, close in, and fasten the Lock, each man drawing his hands apart, passing his right wrist *over* his right neighbour's left hand, and his left wrist *under* his left neighbour's right hand. Still moving clockwise all dance round at the original speed, the Leader holding the Lock in his left hand high above his head, while the rest dance with their hands hanging at their sides. After two or more circuits, at the Leader's discretion, and near the end of a strain of the music, No. 1 lowers the lock to a horizontal position at hip-level. Each man lays hold of the hilt of his own sword with his left hand and, on the middle beat of the last bar, draws it from the Lock.

Figure 2.—The Clap.

At the beginning of the next strain all clash their swords together on the first and middle beats of each bar, as in the Kirkby Malzeard Dance (*see* Part I, p. 44), but much more robustly (8 bars).

All now form a ring, linked hilt-and-point, hands at hip-level, and then, extending arms to their full stretch, dance round clockwise, facing centre so far as the step and movement will allow.

Figure 3.—Threedling (A).

At a signal from the Leader all suddenly halt. Nos. 1 and 8 lower the sword between them (No. 8's), No. 1 making a half-turn clockwise and facing No. 8. The latter then raises his right hand, jumps over his own sword, turns to his left, counter-clockwise, and continues to hold his sword down while Nos. 7, 6, 5, 4, 3 and 2, in order, leap over it, turn to their left and dance round counter-clockwise. Each dancer,

directly he has jumped over the sword, places the tip of his
neighbour's sword over his right (*i.e.*, outside) shoulder.
Whilst Nos. 7, 6, &c., are leaping his sword, No. 8 gradually
moves counter-clockwise round No. 1, until, at the end of the
movement, he is on No. 1's other side, having exchanged places
with No. 2.   During this movement No. 1 gradually makes a
half-turn, counter-clockwise, in order that he may always
face No. 8 ; and, on its completion, stands up, makes a further
half-turn counter-clockwise, and places the tip of No. 8's
sword over his right shoulder :—

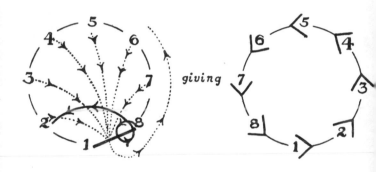

All now dance round counter-clockwise at the original
speed, with the tips of their neighbours' swords over their
right (*i.e.*, outside) shoulders.

Figure 4.—Threedling (B).

After two or more circuits, at the Leader's discretion, the
Leader gives the call and all suddenly halt.   No. 2, passing
his right hand over his head, makes a half-turn counter-
clockwise, and faces No. 1.   Simultaneously, No. 1, raising
his left hand, turns out to his right and, followed by Nos. 8,
7, 6, 5, 4 and 3, dances round clockwise until he is on the
other side of No. 2, having exchanged places with No. 3.

As Nos. 8, 7, &c., successively pass under No. 1's sword they place the tips of their neighbours' swords over their left (*i.e.*, outside) shoulders. At the end of the movement No. 2 does the same:—

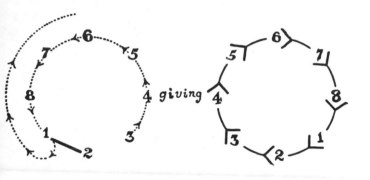

The dancers now dance round, clockwise, in a ring at the original speed, with the tips of their neighbours' swords over their left shoulders.

FIGURE 5.—THREEDLING (C).

After two or more circuits the Leader gives a signal and all suddenly stop. No. 1, passing his right hand over his head, makes a half-turn clockwise, and faces No. 8. Simultaneously, No. 8, passing his right hand over his head, raises his left arm, turns out to his left, followed by Nos. 7, 6, 5, 4, 3 and 2, and dances round counter-clockwise until he is on No. 1's other side, having exchanged places with No. 2. Directly Nos. 7, 6, &c., have passed under No. 8's sword, they place the tips of their neighbours'

swords over their right (*i.e.*, outside) shoulders.   At the end
of the movement No. 1 does the same :—

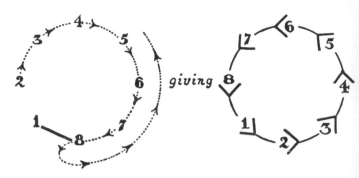

The dancers now dance round, counter-clockwise, in a ring
at the original speed, with the tips of their neighbours' swords
over their right shoulders.

The last two Figures (Threedling, B and C) are now
repeated, alternately, as often as the Leader pleases.   When
he wishes to proceed to the next Figure, the Leader gives a
signal to stop when they are all dancing round (clockwise)
at the close of Figure 4, and when he is at the top of the
room, *i.e.*, at the point nearest the audience.

FIGURE 6.—DOUBLE-THREEDLING (A).

The dancers then separate, release their neighbours' swords,
slope their own over their shoulders, and form two files of
four, facing each other, as in a " longways " Country Dance,
thus :—

		Right file.			
	2	3	4	5	
	V	V	V	V	
Top					Bottom
	Λ	Λ	Λ	Λ	
	1	8	7	6	
		Left file.			

No. 1 now casts off (*i.e.*, turns outward to his left), passes behind Nos. 8, 7 and 6, and dances up the middle to the top; while, at the same time, No. 2 dances down the middle to the bottom, turns out to his left, passes behind Nos. 5, 4 and 3, and dances up to the top. On meeting each other face to face, Nos. 1 and 2 join swords, each grasping the tip of the other's sword with his left hand. They then dance down the middle, "spinning" twice as they go, place themselves at the bottom, below the last couple, unlink swords and slope their own over left shoulders (8 bars). As Nos. 1 and 2 dance down the middle, the other couples move up one place.

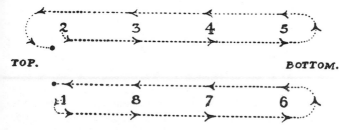

This progressive Figure is then repeated in turn by the remaining three couples, at the conclusion of which all the dancers will be in their original places (32 bars in all).

In "spinning," each dancer of the right file makes a whole-turn on his axis counter-clockwise; while each dancer of the left file makes a whole-turn clockwise.

Dancers when stationary in this and succeeding Figures "mark time" by dancing the skipping-step in their places.

Figure 7.—Double-Threedling (B).

Partners join swords in the way described in the last Figure. The three lower couples form double arches with their swords, under which Nos. 1 and 2 dance down the middle to the bottom, spinning twice as they go (4 bars). During this movement the three arch-couples move up one place (progressive).

This movement is then repeated, in turn, by the remaining three couples, leaving the dancers once again in their original places (**16 bars in all**).

FIGURE 8.—DOUBLE-THREEDLING (C).

All lower their swords to hip-level. The first and second couples now dance the half-pousette (*see* "Country Dance Book," Part II, p. 36), No. 1 first pushing and then pulling his partner (4 bars).

This progressive movement proceeds in the usual Country Dance manner (Duple minor-set). Each couple, upon reaching the top or the bottom, becomes neutral for one change, and spins twice in a stationary position. It will be seen that in going *down* the dance, the left file dancers first push their partners forward and then pull them back ; while in going up the dance, they first pull their partners back and then push them forward. Those belonging to the right file do, of course, the reverse.

This movement is continued at the Leader's pleasure.

FIGURE 9.—THE STRAIGHT HEY.

Choosing a moment when he is at the top, the Leader gives a call. The dancers shoulder their swords and form into single file, all facing up except No. 1, who faces down. The order of the dancers is immaterial ; indeed, for reasons which will presently appear, the more irregular it is the better.

No. 1 then begins a progressive Hey. He passes the first dancer facing him by the right, the next by the left, and so on, each dancer beginning to Hey upwards as No. 1, in his downward course, reaches him, till all are in motion.

Except that the Hey starts progressively, it is, as regards passing, turning at the ends, &c., the ordinary Straight Hey (*see* "Country Dance Book," Part II, p. 45). That is to say, each dancer upon reaching either end of the line, reverses his direction, by making a small loop counter-clockwise, and then, upon re-entering the line, passes the first dancer he meets by the right :—

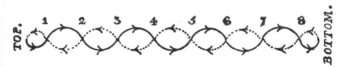

This movement continues as long as the Leader pleases. Choosing a moment when he reaches the top of the line, the Leader, instead of turning back and going down again, falls out three or four yards to either side, and remains stationary, facing up and marking time. When No. 8 reaches the top, he falls out in like manner, stands behind No. 1 and grasps the tip of No. 1's sword with his right hand. Nos. 7, 6, 5, 4, 3 and 2 follow suit, each one placing himself behind the last and grasping the tip of the sword in front of him. In this way a ring is gradually formed. When, finally, No. 2 has linked on to No. 3, No. 1 grasps the tip of No. 2's sword and the circle is complete.

FIGURE 10.—RING-AND-LOCK.

All now dance round in a ring, clockwise, as in the first Figure, and, at a signal from the Leader, tie the Lock. The Leader then raises the Lock in his left hand and faces up, while the rest of the dancers stand in a straight line facing the audience, three on one side of the Leader, four on the other. This brings the dance to a conclusion.

D

NOTATION.

THE BEADNELL SWORD-DANCE.

BEADNELL is a small fishing village situate on the north-east coast of Northumberland, a few miles south of the Farne Islands, and about fifty miles north of Newcastle-on-Tyne. The sword-dance is annually performed there by fishermen on New Year's Day. The dancers, five in number, are accompanied by two Bessies and a musician with an accordion.

COSTUME.

The dancers are dressed in blue jerseys and navy-blue cloth trousers, and wear, over one shoulder and breast, single baldrics or sashes of pink silk or sateen, four or five inches wide, upon which several large rosettes of different colours are sewn. They dance bare-headed.

Each dancer carries a flexible sword or rapper, made of hoop-iron, similar to, but rather longer than, those used by the Swalwell and Earsdon sword-dancers, and without a revolving handle, blocks of wood being fastened on the upper and lower surfaces of each extremity.

The two Bessies are impersonated by men dressed in women's clothes, one of them carrying a red sunshade.

The musician is dressed in his ordinary clothes.

THE MUSIC.

There is no special tune traditionally associated with the dance; the musician chooses any dance air in 6/8 time he thinks suitable.

THE STEP.

Ordinarily the dancers walk or tramp in time with the music, two steps to the bar, but at certain points in the dance, as hereinafter directed, they " step " in the way described in the Grenoside dance (*see* Part I, p. 56).

THE DANCE.

The dance consists of five Figures. As in the Swalwell and Earsdon dances, the movements are continuous, no pause being made between the several evolutions. The locking of the Nut must be completed at the end of one or other strain of the air.

FIGURE 1.

The dancers stand close together in a ring, facing centre, and hold their swords, points up and slanting a little forward, hilts at chin-level, while the musician plays the first strain of the tune (8 bars).

They then perform the following movements :—

(*a.*) The Clash as at Kirkby Malzeard (*see* Part I, p. 44) (8 bars).

(*b.*) Dance round in a ring, clockwise, each dancer placing his sword over his left shoulder and grasping with his left hand the tip of the sword belonging to the man in front of him. The hands are lifted to forehead-level, so that the swords are raised about six inches above the shoulders (8 bars).

(*c.*) One-Turn-Off as at Swalwell (*see* Part I, p. 74).

(*d.*) The Rose. The swords are meshed together in the way that is usual in rapper-dances, that is to say, No. 1 raises his left arm and, followed by Nos. 2, 3 and 4, turns outward to his left (*see* Part I, pp. 74-76). Directly the Nut is formed, it is raised horizontally to breast-level, while the dancers move slowly round, clockwise (8 bars).

(*e.*) All make a half-turn, clockwise, halt, and "step," backs toward centre, hands at shoulder-level (8 bars).

(*f.*) Nos. 1 and 2 each make a half-turn, the former clockwise, the latter counter-clockwise, raise the sword between them, No. 1's, move forward a step or two and pass the sword over the heads of Nos. 3, 4 and 5, who slowly back beneath it. The dancers are now in a ring, facing centre, linked hilt-and-point.

Figure 2.

No. 1 raises his left arm and, followed by Nos. 2 and 3, turns outward to his left and moves round in a small circle, counter-clockwise ; while No. 5 raises his right arm and followed by No. 4 dances round in a circle, clockwise. The dancers in the two circles move round synchronously, Nos. 1 and 5 beginning each fresh circuit, as they face the audience, at the same moment :—

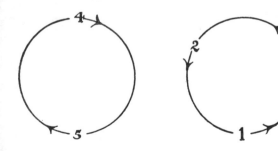

At a call from the Leader, which must be given when he and No. 5 are about to enter upon a new circuit, all face centre, hilt-and-point. No. 1 then turns outward to his left, the Nut is tied, and (*d*), (*e*) and (*f*) are danced as in the first Figure.

FIGURE 3.

The Needle, as at Swalwell (*see* Part I, p. 77).

At its conclusion, the Leader gives the call and all face centre, hilt-and-point; whereupon (*d*), (*e*) and (*f*) follow as in the two preceding Figures.

FIGURE 4.

No. 5 passes under No. 1's sword and, followed by No. 2 proceeds to dance round in a small circle, counter-clockwise; while No. 1 turns outward to his right, passes under his own sword and, followed by Nos. 4 and 3, moves round in a circle, clockwise, thus :—

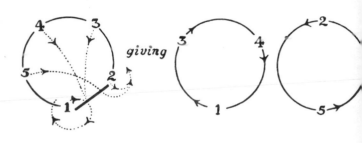

No. 3 may, if he so pleases, change over in successive circuits from one circle to the other, alternately following No. 4 and No. 2.

At a call from the Leader, given when he and No. 5 are beginning a fresh circuit, and when No. 3 is in the left circle, No. 5 backs between Nos. 1 and 3, No. 1 makes a three quarter turn counter-clockwise, and all face centre, hilt-and-point.

The Nut is then tied and (*d*), (*e*) and (*f*) performed as in preceding Figures.

Figure 5.

No. 5 raises his right arm, turns outward to his right and, followed by No. 2, dances round in a circle, clockwise. Directly No. 2 has crossed in front of No. 1, No. 1 raises his left arm, turns outward to his left and, followed by Nos. 4 and 3 (No. 4 in front of No. 3), moves round in a circle, counter-clockwise, thus :—

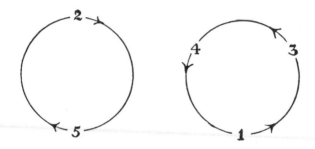

The Leader, at his pleasure, and when he and No. 5 are setting out upon a new circuit, gives the call; whereupon No. 2 moves forward between Nos. 1 and 3 and makes a half-turn, clockwise.

No. 1 then turns out to his left, the Nut is tied, and the Rose danced as in the first Figure. On the conclusion of the Rose, No. 1 raises the Nut in his right hand, high above his head, and faces audience, the rest of the dancers forming up in a straight line and facing in the like direction, Nos. 5 and 4 on No. 1's right, Nos. 2 and 3 on his left.

This concludes the dance.

THE HANDSWORTH SWORD DANCERS.

THE

SWORD DANCES

OF

NORTHERN ENGLAND

COLLECTED AND DESCRIBED

BY

CECIL J. SHARP.

2nd Edition, 1951, revised by
MAUD KARPELES

———

PART III.

———

PREFACE.

My most cordial thanks are due, first of all, to the dancers from whom the technical information contained in the following pages has been derived, more especially to Messrs. John Siddall and Ernest Shaw, of Handsworth; Mr. George Wright, of Darlington (late of Ampleforth); Mr. S. Bland, of Askham Richard; Mr. T. Daker, of Haxby; Mr. William Prudhoe, of Winlaton; and Mr. W. Clark, of Walbottle.

I wish also to acknowledge the friendly assistance which, in the course of my investigations, I have received from Mrs. Place, Sir Benjamin Browne, Rev. C. Trollope, Mr. Hugh Fairfax-Cholmeley, Mr. J. Ronksley, Mr. A. Butterworth, Mr. Duncan Naish, Mr. Parker Brewis, and Mr. Barry Jones.

Finally, I would thank Mr. George Butterworth for helping me to collect three of the dances; and, once again, my good friend Mr. E. Phillips Barker for criticising and amending my MS., reading the proofs, and in countless ways aiding me in the preparation of my book.

C. J. S.

Uxbridge, 1913.

CONTENTS.

CHAPTER II.

THE SHORT SWORD DANCE.

INTRODUCTION.

THE five long-sword dances described in the following pages were collected at the following villages in Yorkshire :—Escrick, Handsworth, Ampleforth, Askham Richard, and Haxby; and the two short-sword or rapper dances at Winlaton (Co. Durham) and Walbottle (Northumberland).

Further research in Yorkshire has shown that as recently as twenty-five years ago sword-dancing was very generally practised as a Christmas pastime, if not throughout the whole county, certainly in that part of it which lies east of a line drawn through Redcar, Thirsk, and Sheffield.

I have found, too, that the dance varies in type with different districts, and not, like the Morris dance of the Midlands, village by village. For the purposes of publication I have therefore had to select the best and most typical example from each locality or group of villages. This has necessitated the rejection of dances collected at Helmsley, Kirkby Moorside, Skelton-in-Cleveland, and Poppleton. An extremely interesting dance that used to be performed at Thirsk I have had reluctantly to omit because I failed to elicit from the three surviving members of the team full and trustworthy information respecting its movements.

Three only of the seven dances described in this volume — the Handsworth, Winlaton, and Walbottle dances—are still annually performed; so that for my information respecting the remaining four I have had to trust to the memories of individual dancers, survivors of their respective teams, nearly all of which were disbanded upwards of a quarter of a century ago.

In the Introductions to Parts I. and II. two conclusions concerning the origin and meaning of the sword dance were arrived at : (1) That the dance originally formed part of a ceremony quasi-religious or magical in character, the purport of which was to promote the fertility of the soil and of all living things ; (2) That the central ritual act was the killing and subsequent restoration to life of a man who, from the character of his dress and other considerations, represented, apparently, the animal world.

It will be recalled that a great part of the argument turned upon the interpretation of one particular figure of the dance, namely that in which the swords are locked together round the neck of one of the extra characters and then simultaneously withdrawn by the dancers. The conclusion ultimately reached was that this act denoted a killing or mimic decapitation. Any doubt which remained as to the accuracy of this deduction is removed by the additional evidence supplied by several of the dances described in the following pages. In the Askham Richard dance, for instance, when the swords are withdrawn from the Lock, which is placed round the Fool's neck, the Fool falls to the ground, feigns death, and is subsequently restored to life by the Besom Betty. A similar incident forms the climax of the Haxby dance ; while in the Ampleforth variant the death and revival of the victim form the subject of a lengthy dramatic dialogue. Again, at Escrick, when the swords are released from the Lock and Woody falls to the ground, his hat is tipped off by one of the dancers, and this, I was told, was done expressly to emphasise his death. What the dancers themselves believe is clear enough, because they habitually talk about it as " killing the Clown."

It should be mentioned that in two cases the doctor, who is summoned to restore the dead man to life, fails in his task, and the revival is effected by, respectively, the Clown and the Besom Betty.

Properly to understand the full significance of this curious ceremony, one must remember that in the earliest stages of his history primitive man drew no clear distinction between himself, the group or tribe to which he belonged, and other living things, vegetable or animal. This inability to individualise himself, to differentiate himself, either in thought or feeling, from any of the various forms of life, human, animal, or plant, by which he was surrounded, found its expression in his totemistic cult. For totemism means the selection by the tribe of another, non-human group, *e.g.*, one particular species of animal or plant, with which it assumed a close relationship. So intimate, indeed, was this feeling of kinship between human and non-human groups, that at first it amounted to one of identity. Gradually, however, as his mental powers increased, man began dimly to distinguish between himself and his totem. This, however, so far from leading him to emphasise the growing feeling of separation, seems rather to have impelled him to preserve and strengthen the bond by artificial and magical means. To this end he felt it necessary periodically to slaughter his totem animal, to partake sacramentally of its flesh and, by thus absorbing the animal *mana*, to identify his own life with the energies of a more potent vitality. Such an act as this, involving the deliberate killing of his totem, which was of course *tabu* to him, was not lightly to be undertaken ; nor was it one which could safely or with propriety be done by an individual. The sacrifice had therefore to be performed communally, either by the whole tribe or, in its name, by certain deputed individuals.

Again, food being man's primary need, his chief attention was centred upon those natural phenomena which appeared to him to control or influence the growth and increase of the plants and animals upon which his material existence depended. He perceived that the scheme of nature was a rhythmical one ; that season followed season in orderly sequence ; that each period of growth was succeeded by one of decay, to be followed, in due course, by a period of renewed life. And thus he came to realise that decay or death was a condition precedent to a renewal of vitality ; that Winter must precede Spring, just as night must come before day, and sleep before a restoration of his physical and mental faculties.

Hence the need was felt of actively doing something to promote this scheme, especially at that period of the year, in mid-winter, when the forces of nature were at their lowest ebb. The resulting rite was based upon the principle of mimetic magic, the conception that like produced like and that a desired effect could be attained by imitating it. In this particular case, therefore, the magic rite took the form of a mock death followed by a mock resurrection, in imitation of the cyclic death of the Old Year and the rebirth of the New.

Now in the Sword dance, traces of both of these ritual acts or *dromena* are still to be found—the slaughter and perhaps the sacramental eating of the totem animal, and the dramatic representation of the death and resurrection of the year.

In the Midland Morris dance, which is closely related to, if not an actual offshoot of, the Sword dance, the accompanying ceremony of killing an animal and afterwards feasting upon it has already been noticed (see *The Morris Book*, Part I., 2nd Edition, pp. 25-27).

It is true that, so far as investigation has yet been carried, no extant sword dance provides a specific instance of the actual slaughter of an animal. The animal insignia, however, sometimes attached (originally doubtless as a vehicle of *mana**) to the central figure of a mimic execution seems to imply the antecedence of such a sacrifice. At Sleights, too, and at Askham Richard, Sowerby, and other places, it was customary for the sword dancers at the conclusion of their season to feast together, and this, it may be, contains the last relic of the primitive sacramental meal.

The symbolic representation of the death of the Old Year and the rebirth of the New, performed with the intent to

---

* This may be taken as a correction of the less probable view expressed in Part I. (p. 33) on the animalization of the Captain at Grenoside.

bring about the desired sequence of seasons, is, however, plainly to be seen in the sword dance. In three of the Yorkshire dances, presently to be described, the Fool or Clown is killed and afterwards restored to life; while at Ampleforth, where the dance is set in the midst of a long dramatic dialogue, this is brought out very strongly. For here we have something more than a bald enaction of a mock death and resurrection. The drama opens with the courting of the Queen by the King at the instigation of the Clown, his father. Before, however, the wooing has reached the desired consummation, the action is interrupted by the entrance of the dancers, who, at the conclusion of their dance, kill a man and flee in consternation from the stage. After a formal denial of complicity in the murder on the part of each individual dancer, a lamentation over the dead man and a comic funeral service, a doctor is summoned to restore the corpse to life. As he fails, however, to do this, the Clown intervenes and restores the dead man; whereupon the dancers resume their performance and the entertainment is brought to a conclusion.

The Ampleforth Play is an exceedingly interesting survival. It is, of course, a form, if a crude and somewhat corrupt one, of the "Folk-Play," of which the Revesby Play is another and well-known English example. (See *Folk-lore Journal*, vii., 1889, p. 377.) Several examples of this ancient folk-drama are still to be found in Europe. For a typical example we may cite one which is still annually performed in Thrace at Haghios Gheorghios and the neighbourhood. The chief incidents in this play, which has been most carefully noted by Mr. Dawkins,* are as follows : A baby, borne in a cradle by an old woman (the Babo), is supposed, in the course of the early part of the play, to grow up to man's estate. He demands a wife, and pursues one of the female characters, a man-woman. After a mock marriage ceremony between them has been performed, the bridegroom is killed with a bow

---

* *Journal of Hellenic Studies*, vol. xxvi. (1906) pp. 190-206.

by his comrade, who had previously acted as best-man at the marriage. The wife throws herself across the prostrate body and laments the death of her lover with loud cries, the slayer and the rest of the actors joining in and " making a regular parody of a Christian burial, burning dung as incense and pretending to sing the service." Whereupon the dead man suddenly comes alive again and gets up, thus ending his part of the play.

There are other incidents in the play, *e.g.*, the scattering of seed, the forging and construction of a plough-share, which, after the revival of the murdered victim, is drawn in procession round the ground (*cf.* the Plough Stots at Sleights and elsewhere), &c., &c., all of which indicate that the object of the ceremony is to ensure the fertilization of the crops. Both the bridegroom and his murderer are animalized and disguised in a head-dress formed of an entire goat-skin without the horns, which, falling over the face and neck, forms a mask, with holes cut for the eyes and mouth. Their hands are blackened and sheep-bells are worn around their waists (*cf.* the blackened faces of the Sleights dancers, Part II., pp. 13-14 ; and the costume of the Kirkby Malzeard Fool, Part I., p. 40). In addition to the characters already named, there is a second man-woman dressed like the bride, three or more Gipsy smiths, who make the plough-share, two or three young men, policemen, carrying swords and whips, and a musician who plays the bagpipes.

The drama, it should be added, opens with a hand-in-hand dance of all the characters, the policemen brandishing their drawn swords ; while the evening is spent in feasting on the presents collected during the day.

The likeness to the Ampleforth Play is obvious. In both dramas we have a hand-in-hand dance in a ring with the brandishing of swords ; a marriage or courtship between two characters, one of whom is dressed in woman's clothes ; the killing of a man who has miraculously grown up in the course of the Play * ; a lamentation and mock funeral service ; the restoration to life of the slain man ; and finally, on th' conclusion of the ceremony, a communal feast.

Mr. Wace, from several scattered and fragmentary festivals, constructs the full original as follows † :—

" The old woman first appears nursing her baby in her arms, and this child is, in some way or other, peculiar. He grows up quickly and demands a bride. A bride is found for him, and the wedding is celebrated, but during the wedding festivities he quarrels with one of his companions, who attempts to molest the bride, and is killed. He is then lamented by his bride, and miraculously restored to life. The interrupted festivities are resumed, and the marriage is consummated."

Mr. Gilbert Murray maintains‡ that Greek Tragedy is in origin a Ritual Dance, a Sacer Ludus ; and that this dance is originally or centrally that of Dionysus an " Eniautos-Daimon," who represents the cyclic death and rebirth of the world, including the rebirth of the tribe by the return of the heroes or dead ancestors. Mr. Murray further summarises the incidents which underlie the various " Eniautos " celebrations as follows :—

1. An *Agon* or Contest, the Year against its Enemy, Light against Darkness, Summer against Winter.

2. A *Pathos* of the Year-Daimon, generally a ritual or sacrificial death.

3. A *Messenger* who announces the news of the death.

4. A *Threnos* or Lamentation, with, as its special characteristic, a clash of emotions, the death of the old being also the triumph of the new.

5. An *Anagnorisis*—discovery or recognition—of the slain and mutilated Daimon, followed by his Resurrection or Apotheosis.

---

* *See* p. 72.

† *Annual of the British School at Athens*, No. xvi., p. 251, quoted in Miss J. E. Harrison's *Themis*, p. 332.

‡ *Excursus on the Ritual Forms preserved in Greek Tragedy*, printed in Miss J. E. Harrison's *Themis*, pp. 341-363.

(2) (4) and (5) are all of course to be found in the Ampleforth Play.

(1), however, is absent, unless we see, in the quarrel (in Part II.) for the Queen's hand, the contest between Winter (the Clown) and Spring (the King). (3), too, is wanting, but here again the dancers' denial of complicity in the murder may perhaps be regarded as a formal announcement of the death.

It has even been maintained* that a similar ritual scheme lies at the foundation of one of Shakespeare's plays, "The Winter's Tale," in the contest between Leontes and Hermione, leading to their alienation and the supposed death of the latter; the loss of Perdita; the remorse of Leontes; the discovery of Perdita; and the return to life of Hermione—all of which, it is contended, is but a personified representation of the yearly life of the earth, its winter death, and spring resurrection, made doubly clear by the title of the play.

Incredible as it may at first seem, we have, then, in the folk-play, of which our Ampleforth dance is an example, the ritual-form upon which, as upon a warp, was woven the rich fabric of Attic drama. But, lest the case be over-stated, let us remember that it was the form only, not its content, which the Greek Tragedy owed to the primitive fertilization ceremony.

Interesting as the Ampleforth play undoubtedly is from a historical or folk-lore point of view, it cannot be said that artistically it stands on the same level with the sword dance with which it was mated. Some of the " patter " or fooling, rhyming tags, quaint primitive expressions, bits of song and so on are quite lively and good in their way. But regarded as a whole, the texture is so coarse and rough, and in many places incoherent, and the bald, stupid passages so frequent that the artistic effect is negligible. Why is it, it may be asked, that the folk, who attained to such a high

---

* See *Bacon, Shakespeare, and the Rosicrucians,* ch. vii., by Mr. W. F. C. Wigston.

artistic level in their songs, music, and dances, failed so egregiously in the domain of drama ? Fortunately, the answer to this need not now detain us. The question does not really arise, because the Ampleforth play is obviously not a pure folk-product. It needs but a cursory glance at the text to see that it has been subjected to many influences, and that many hands have been at work upon it. Several lines for instance have been " lifted " from Congreve's " Love for Love," * and there is no doubt that many authors, good, bad, and indifferent, have in like manner been drawn upon. Exactly what its history has been we can but speculate.

Roughly, however, as Mr. Phillips Barker has suggested, it must have been something of the following nature :—

" First there is the sword dance as a seasonal ceremony and (probably a separate ceremony but becoming attached to the sword dance as belonging to the same season) a very primitive form of masking, setting forth, probably in dumb show, unless there were rude chants of joy or sorrow interjected, the life and death of the year-daimon. In the second stage the sword dance and the masking are caught up into civic life. The guilds use them ; they are for the time fashionable entertainments. The effect on the masking is noticeable ; it becomes a play, words are written, it has dialogue, clowning, and so on. All this development is, however, not what one can call *folk*, but *popular*—a very different thing. It belongs to a culture which is not that of the peasant, whether it be better or worse. Clerics or secular scholars supply texts ; quick-witted craftsmen act them. The elaborated dramatic form, helped by the interest of the cultured or semi-cultured classes, spreads from the towns, and in most cases ousts the old rude beginnings.

" Then comes the third stage. The townsman loses interest in this kind of entertainment—the guilds drop it ; sword dance

---

* *Cf.* lines 43-4, 54-60, and 73-76, First Part, with Congreve's " Love for Love," Act iii., Sc. 3.

and play again belong to the peasant only, who being a good
man of his hands and feet is equal to all the complexity of
the dance, but cannot maintain at its original level that part
of the entertainment which is an intrusion from an alien
culture.　Hence the dance proceeds with little degeneration;
the play gradually loses form, meaning, and coherency."

It may be that it is mainly on account of its artistic
superiority that the dance has outlived the play.　That either
should have survived till now is wonderful enough, especially
when we remember that it must be a thousand years at least
since the performers of either sword dance or play have
attached any religious significance to their acts beyond "at
most "—as Mr. E. K. Chambers has pointed out—"holding it
to be 'for luck,' and in some vague general way to the
interest of a fruitful year in field and fold." *

---

* *The Mediæval Stage*, i., p. 94.

CHAPTER I.

THE LONG-SWORD DANCE.

THE ESCRICK SWORD DANCE.

Escrick is a small village about five miles south of York. A sword dance used to be performed there annually at Christmas-time until forty years ago, when it fell into disuse. There were eleven performers—the Clown, Madam Sylvester (the Clown's wife), King, Queen, Woody, and six dancers.

COSTUME.

The dancers wore white calico tunics with crimson collars and cuffs, and epaulets of different-coloured wools; breeches of white or light-coloured cord; white stockings and low shoes; and high silk hats decorated with ribbons and artificial flowers, with four sprigs of ivy or holly with gilded berries fixed round the outer edge of the crown. The hats were not, of course, worn during the performance.

The Clown had a gay coat, the body of which differed in colour from the sleeves, and the sleeves from each other; breeches; stockings of different colours; and a gay cap with a fox's tail hanging from the back of it. Woody had a loose-fitting white jacket trimmed with ribbons; wide trousers; and a cap similar to that worn by the Clown.

The King was very smartly dressed in his best clothes.

The Queen was impersonated by a man, dressed in woman's clothes.

Madam Sylvester — sometimes called the Betty or Besom-Betty—was a man-woman, carrying a broom, and dressed like a witch in a bonnet, shawl, and patched skirt.

Each dancer carried a well-made steel sword, the blade of which was thirty-one inches long by an inch-and-an-eighth wide at the hilt, tapering to the point. The hilt, six inches in length, was made of dark wood very neatly shaped and turned, with a brass knob at the top. A tassel was fastened to the lower part of the hilt of each sword, each man having his own distinctive colour, so that he might recognise his sword in the Lock.

THE MUSIC.

The music, which was played by the village band, consisted of a song-air, used in the Prologue, and two dance tunes "The Fisher Laddie" and "The Oyster Girl" (see "Sword Dance Songs and Dance Airs," Book III.).

A slight pause is made at the conclusion of each figure. The music in each figure is continuous, and—except when otherwise directed—controls the steps only. In Figures 1 2 and 3, the Clash, and the first movement of the Rose, are each accompanied with the first strain (A) of the music. The musician must remember to accompany the third movement of the Rose in Figure 3 with B music.

THE STEP.

In the Lock, the Rose, and Meet-and-cross, the dancers march or walk. Throughout the rest of the dance, except where otherwise directed, they use a quiet, running step something betwixt a walk and a run. This, at least, is all that I could gather from Mr. Bell, who—owing to his great age—was unable to do more than describe the movement.

THE PROCESSION.

In going from one station to another the company marched in the following order:—The band, Clown and Madam Sylvester, Woody, King and Queen, and the six dancers in single file, each holding his sword erect in front of him, hilt at chin level, with a coloured handkerchief on the point like a flag.

THE DANCE.

PROLOGUE.

[Enter Clown, who bows to the audience.

Clown :   With your leave, kind gentlemen,
    Of you I'll take a view ;
    Our actors are a-coming in ;
    They will be here enoo.*
    I was condemned to die,
    As I've heard people say,
    But I got my reprieve, so I
    Came jogging on this way.
    My old Grand-ma was a witch,
    As I've heard people speäk,
    She rode a-hunting on our black bitch
    To yonder corner neäk.†
    We have got no family,
    None can compare to mine ;
    My father he was hanged
    For stealing of a swine.
    My father he was hanged,
    My mother drowned in a well,
    And isn't I a hopeful chuck
    Just here alive to tell ?

---

* Presently, soon.   † Nook.

So, your servant, gentlemen,
I've got no more to say :
Our actors are a-comin' in
I'll draw 'em on this way.

CALLING-ON SONG.

[*No.* 1 *enters, bows to the Clown, places his
sword over his right shoulder, and
walks round in a small circle, clockwise,
followed by the Clown, who sings as
follows :*

Clown :   The first that does enter is a noble, brave Knight ;
(*Sings*)   He's a man of much breeding and fame,
He ventured his life for the sake of a wife,
And Sir Thomas Dollymore is his name.

[*At the beginning of each of the following
five stanzas, the remaining five dancers
enter in succession as they are called,
bow to the Clown, shoulder swords, and
march round in front of him and
behind the last dancer.*   *After each
stanza, which is sung unaccompanied,
the band plays the tune once through
while the dancers and the Clown
march round.*

Clown :   The next is a hero so stout and so bold,
(*Sings*)   He conquers wherever he goes,
He scorns by his enemies to be controlled,
And his name is Sir William Rose.

The next is a merchant, that trades on the sea ;
Much money he's got on the main ;
He's been in far countries for riches, you see,
And now he's returned back again.

The next is a gentleman of high renown ;
Of him I'm afraid of my life,
For he went a-wooing last midsummer's eve,
And won my sweetheart for his wife.

The next is Burgallis, as we do him call ;
He 's a General under our King,
And with his broad dagger he makes them to fall ;
Isn't that a most valiant thing ?

The next is young Trimbush, that witty young spark,
Which never no one can excel ;
He 's a comical lad, and takes after his dad,
And pleases the young ladies right well.

> [*At the conclusion of the last stanza, and
> while the band is playing the tune for
> the last time, the six dancers form up in
> line, facing the audience, the Clown
> standing at the side, thus :*

6	5	4	3	2	1
V	V	V	V	V	V

Clown. Audience.

> [*Enter Madam Sylvester, who bows to the
> Clown.*

Clown : In comes old Madam Sylvester,
(Speaks) My blest confounded wife ;
She 's been a plague to me
All the days of my living life.
Let me go where'er I will,
Through city, house, or town,
She follows me in full cry
Like a pack of saucy hounds.
If you wish to know my name

That before they did me call,
I was once as fine a gentleman
As any of you all.
But now this wedding's brought me down
And made of me a fool,
I'm no more like to what I was
Than a pig is like an owl.

> [*The band plays the song-air once through,*
>   *while Woody enters and makes his*
>   *obeisance to the Clown.*

Clown :   Here's Woody Garius I'd like to forgot,
(Sings) His beauty's so much like my own ;
           But if ever I get his fat head to the pot,
           I'll make it strike fourteen at noon.

> [*The band plays the song-air, during which*
>   *the King and Queen enter and bow to*
>   *the Clown.*

Clown :   As for myself I must drive up the rear,
(Sings) My name unto you I'll relate ;
           I spent all my money by hunting bold Renny,
           And it's I, Sirs, they call Mr. Tate.
           But my name it is Mr. Foxtails ; foxtails
           Are fair on my back to be seen ;
           Although my old clothes are ragged and torn
           I once was beloved by a Queen.
           Some calls me a King, some calls me a Clown ;
           My valour I'll never deny,
           For I once killed a hedgehog as big as myself,
           And it made me a rare apple-pie.
           So now, bonny ladies, I bid you farewell,
           I wish you no manner of ill,
           I wish you all sweethearts, and I two new coats,
           And, my ladies, I bid you farewell.

> [*The Clown bustles about while Madam*
>   *Sylvester sweeps the ground with the*
>   *broom.*

Clown :   Make room, gentlemen, make room I pray,

(Speaks)   We'll show you all the sport we can before we go away.

> Our actors are but young, they never acted on the stage before,
>
> But they mean to do the best they can and the best can do no more.
>
> But since it's been my lot to fall here by chance,
> I've got six lively lads shall dance you the sword-dance ;
> They will be here enoo, if you be wisht and still,
> This very day they intend to dance "T'Old Wife of Coverdill."

> > [*The Clown and the extra characters now move to the side, while the band strikes up " The Fisher Laddie" and the dancers begin the following figures.*

FIGURE 1.

Music.	Movements.
A1 1—4	THE CLASH.
	Nos. 1 and 6 leave the ranks and walk round in a small circle, clockwise, holding their swords in their right hands, points up, hilts at chin-level, and clashing them together on the first and middle beats of each bar.
5—8	Each dancer makes a half-turn, counter-clockwise, changes his sword into his left hand, and walks back to his place, clashing as before. At the close of the movement each changes his sword back into his right hand.

Music.	Movements.

Swing-and-Spin.

B1   1—4

Nos. 1 and 6 now face each other, No. 1 with the audience on his left, each grasping the tip of the other's sword. With straight arms, they now swing their swords to and fro, alternately away from and toward the audience, on the first and middle beats of the first two bars. The motion is like that of two men swinging a heavy sack preparatory to heaving it on to a wagon. In the following two bars they spin (*see* Part II., pp. 26 and 35) once round, No. 1 clockwise, No. 6 counter-clockwise.

  5—8

These two movements are now repeated in reverse directions, the dancers first swinging toward the audience, and spinning, No. 1 counter-clockwise, No. 6 clockwise.

The Clash.

A2   1—8

Nos. 2 and 5 now leave the ranks and join Nos. 1 and 6. All four dancers clash as in A1, standing in the following order :—

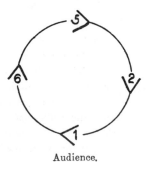

Audience.

Music.	Movements.

Swing-and-Spin.

B2   1—4

The four dancers now stand thus, each grasping with his left hand the tip of his partner's sword :—

$$5 =\!=\!=\!=\!=\!=\!=\!= 2$$

$$6 =\!=\!=\!=\!=\!=\!=\!= 1$$

Audience.

Both couples now swing and spin as in B1, Nos. 1 and 6 as before, Nos. 2 and 5 in the reverse directions.

    5—8

These two movements are then repeated, each couple swinging and spinning in the opposite directions.

The Clash.

A3   1—8

Nos. 3 and 4 now join the other four dancers, and all clash as in A2, No. 3 standing behind No. 2, and No. 4 behind No. 3, thus :—

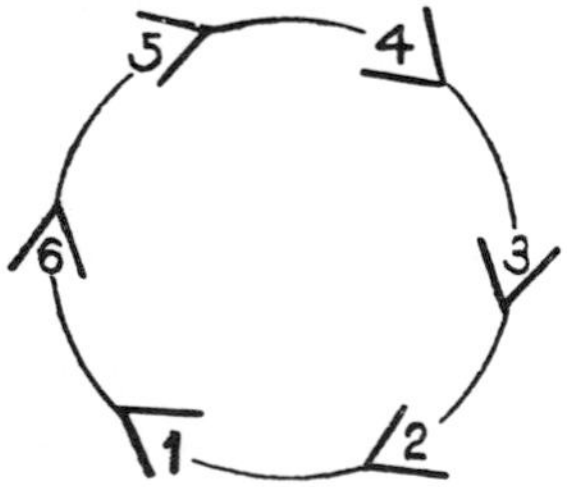

Audience.

Music.	Movements.

Swing-and-Spin.

B3 1—8

The dancers now stand thus, each dancer grasping the tip of his partner's sword with his left hand :—

$$4 \textequals 3$$

$$5 \textequals 2$$

$$6 \textequals 1$$

Audience.

The three couples now swing and spin as in B2, Nos. 3 and 4 duplicating the movements, respectively, of Nos. 1 and 6.

The Clash.

A1 1—8

The six dancers now stand in a ring, face clockwise, and clash as in the preceding figure —that is, all march eight steps clockwise, hold their swords in their right hands and clash them together in time with the music (four bars) ; make a half-turn, counter-clockwise, change swords into left hands, and walk back eight steps, counter-clockwise, to places, clashing as before (four bars). At the close of this movement they change their swords into their right hands again.

Music.	Movements.

Left-over-Right-Lock.

B1 1—8   All move round, clockwise, in hilt and point formation, close in, and lock the swords together, each crossing left wrist over right and bending the hilt of his sword over the point of the sword adjacent to it. This is similar to the Kirkby Lock (see Part I., p. 52), except that wrists are crossed *left over right*, and hilts bent *over* points.

The Rose.

A2 1—4   All walk round eight steps, clockwise, the leader raising the Lock above his head in his right hand, arm erect.

5—8   All make a half-turn counter-clockwise and return to places, the leader changing the Lock into his left hand.

B2 1—4   The leader lowers the Lock to a horizontal position, shoulder-level, and all march round eight steps clockwise, each holding the hilt of his own sword in his right hand.

5—8   Still holding the swords in their right hands, all make a half-turn, clockwise, and walk back eight steps to places. On the middle beat of the last bar all draw their swords from the Lock by a smart back-handed movement, arms bent at the elbows and level with shoulders, swords horizontal, points toward centre of the ring, each man slightly turning, or swinging, clockwise.

FIGURE 2.

THE CLASH.

As in Figure 1 (last time).

UNDER-SINGLE.

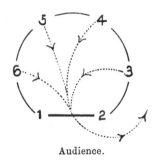

Audience.

All link up, hilt-and-point. Nos. 1 and 2 form an arch with No. 1's sword; both make a three-quarter turn under the raised sword, No. 1 clockwise, No. 2 counter-clockwise, and stand back to back. Nos. 1 and 2 now stand still while Nos. 3, 4, 5, and 6, pass, in turn, under the arch, turn to their left and return to places, No. 4 passing behind No. 3, No. 5 behind Nos. 3 and 4, and No. 6 behind Nos. 3, 4, and 5. As No. 6 goes to his place he passes his sword, with the aid of No. 1, over the heads of all the other dancers.

This movement is then repeated five times, Nos. 2, 3, 4, 5, and 6, in turn, raising their swords.

After the completion of the last round, if Nos. 1 and 2 are not in position (*i.e.*, with their backs to the audience) all move round, clockwise, until the discrepancy is rectified, when they scrape the tips of their swords on the ground in time with the music, moving them alternately from right to left and left to right, until the end of the strain of the music.

The Clash.

As in Figure 1 (last time).

Over-Single.

All link up, hilt-and-point. No. 1, having lowered his sword, jumps over it, raising his left arm and making a three-quarter turn clockwise. Simultaneously, No. 2, raising his right arm, jumps over the lowered sword, making a three-quarter turn, counter-clockwise. Nos. 3, 4, 5, and 6 successively jump over No. 1's sword, turn to their left round No. 2, and return to places as in Under-single. No. 1, immediately No. 6 has jumped over his sword, stands up and with a circular sweep of his left arm passes No. 6's sword over the heads of all the other dancers.

This movement is then repeated five times, Nos. 2, 3, 4, 5, and 6 successively lowering their swords.

After the completion of the last round the dancers adjust their position (if necessary), halt, and scrape their swords on the ground as above described.

The Clash.

As in Figure 1 (last time).

Woody Lock.

All link up, hilt-and-point. Woody now enters the ring, and the dancers make the Back-lock round Woody's neck, in the same way as in the Sleights dance (*see* Part II., p. 22), except that each man passes his sword behind his right-hand neighbour, *shoulder*-high, and the dancers, instead of raising their hands over their heads, bend down and pass their heads beneath their swords (8 bars, B music).

The Rose.

As in Figure 1. When, however, the swords are drawn, the leader knocks off Woody's hat with the tip of his sword, Woody falls to the ground, as though dead, and then rolls out of the ring.

FIGURE 3.

The Clash.

As in Figure 1 (last time).

Under-Double.

All line up, hilt-and-point. Nos. 1 and 2 hold up No. 1's sword and make each a three-quarter turn under the raised sword, No. 1 clockwise, No. 2 counter-clockwise, and stand back to back. Nos. 6 and 3 pass under the arch, side by side, followed by Nos. 5 and 4, and all return to places, Nos. 6 and 5 turning to their right round No. 1 (No. 5 passing behind No. 6), and Nos. 3 and 4 to their left round No. 2 (No. 4 passing behind No. 3).

This movement is then repeated five times, Nos. 2, 3, 4, 5, and 6 successively holding up their swords.

At the completion of the last round the dancers adjust their position (if necessary), halt, and scrape their swords on the ground as above described.

The Clash.

As in Figure 1 (last time).

Over-Double.

All link up, hilt-and-point. No. 1 lowers his sword, whereupon Nos. 1 and 2, raising left and right arms respectively, jump over it, each making a three-quarter turn, No. 1 clockwise, No. 2 counter-clockwise. Nos. 6 and 3 side by side, followed by Nos. 5 and 4, then leap over the sword, and return to places, Nos. 6 and 5 turning to their right (No. 5 passing behind No. 6), and Nos. 3 and 4 to their left (No. 4 passing behind No. 3).

This movement is then repeated five times, Nos. 2, 3, 4, 5, and 6 successively lowering their swords.

At the completion of the last round the dancers adjust their position (if necessary), halt, and scrape their swords on the ground as already described.

THE CLASH.

As in Figure 1 (last time).

SHOULDER-LOCK.

All form ring, facing counter-clockwise, place swords over right shoulders and grasp with left hands the tips of the swords in front. They move round slowly, and then, at a word from the leader, make a three-quarter turn clockwise, face centre, and make a Lock, bending points beneath hilts (8 bars, B music).

THE ROSE.

At the beginning of the next strain the Lock is exhibited in the way already described (8 bars, A music).

The leader then places the locked swords on the ground in the centre of the ring, and each man, facing the hilt of his own sword, " steps " (8 bars, B music).

The leader then raises the Lock to a horizontal position, shoulder-high, all march round, clockwise and counter-clockwise, and draw their swords in the way described in Figure 1 (8 bars, B music).

FIGURE 4.

MEET-AND-CROSS.

The dancers place their swords over right shoulders, and stand in two files, facing one another, thus .

```
4 >      < 3
5 >      < 2
6 >      < 1
```

Audience.

Music.		Movements.
A1	1—2	The two files advance four steps, partners clashing their swords together in the middle beat of the second bar.
	3—4	All retire four steps backward to places.
	5—8	The same again.
B1	1—4	As in A1.
	5—8	Partners pass by the right, change places, make a half-turn clockwise, and face one another.
A2	1—8	As in A1.
B2	1—8	As in B1, to places.

PLAITING.

Each dancer grasps the tip of his partner's sword with his left hand, thus:

Bottom.

4 ═══════════ 3

5 ═══════════ 2

6 ═══════════ 1

Top.

Audience.

They then perform the half-pousette as in the Flamborough dance (*see* Part II., p. 36) until all are once again in their original positions (24 bars). Neutral couples at either end should always spin, left-file dancers counter-clockwise, right-file clockwise. This movement is repeated as often as the leader elects.

The Roll.

Nos. 1 and 6 raise their swords and move down, changing places with Nos. 2 and 5, who move up under the swords held by Nos. 1 and 6. Nos. 1 and 6 then change places with Nos. 3 and 4, passing under the swords held by the latter; while Nos. 2 and 5 spin, No. 5 clockwise, No. 2 counterclockwise. This process is continued, each couple moving from one end to the other and back again, always passing *over* the middle couple and *under* the top or bottom couple, and spinning upon reaching either end.

This movement is repeated as long as the leader elects. When the dancers are all in their original positions, the leader gives the word and all form a ring, Nos. 1 and 2 with their backs to the audience, and wait until the end of the strain, scraping their swords on the ground.

The New Roll.

All link up, hilt-and-point, while Nos. 1 and 2 hold up the sword between them. Nos. 3 and 6, side by side, followed by Nos. 4 and 5, then pass under the raised sword, Nos. 6 and 5 turning to their left and moving round No. 2, Nos. 3 and 4 to their right and round No. 1, No. 3 passing in front of No. 6, and No. 4 in front of No. 5. Simultaneously, Nos. 1 and 2 make each a whole-turn, No. 1 clockwise, No. 2 counterclockwise. The four dancers now pass again under the sword, Nos. 6 and 5 moving round No. 2, Nos. 3 and 4 round No. 1, and repeat the process as often as the leader elects.

In the last round Nos. 6 and 5 turn to their right round No. 1, and Nos. 3 and 4 to their left round No. 2, No. 6 passing behind No. 3, and No. 5 behind No. 4. Upon reaching their places the dancers, now in hilt-and-point formation, face centre, move round to position, halt there and scrape their swords on the ground to and fro as above described. Throughout this movement, which is a very difficult one, the dancers must keep their hands close together and high above their heads.

This concludes the dance.

NOTATION.

Fig. 1.   The Clash (*see* p. 25).
Swing-and Spin (*see* p. 26).
The Clash (*see* p. 26).
Swing and-Spin (*see* p. 27).
The Clash (*see* p. 27).
Swing and-Spin (*see* p. 28).
The Clash (*see* p. 28).
Left over-right Lock (*see* p. 29).
The Rose (*see* p. 29).

Fig. 2.   The Clash (*see* p. 28).
Under-Single (*see* p. 30).
The Clash (*see* p. 28).
Over-Single (*see* p. 31).
The Clash (*see* p. 28).
Woody Lock (*see* p. 31).
The Rose (*see* p. 31).

Fig. 3.   The Clash (*see* p. 28 .
Under-Double (*see* p. 32).
The Clash (*see* p. 28).
Over-Double (*see* p. 32).
The Clash (*see* p. 28).
Shoulder Lock (*see* p. 33).
The Rose (*see* p. 33).

Fig. 4.   Meet-and-Cross (*see* p. 33).
Plaiting (*see* p. 34).
The Roll (*see* p. 35).
The New Roll (*see* p. 35).

THE HANDSWORTH SWORD DANCE.

HANDSWORTH is a populous suburb of Sheffield. The dance originally belonged to Woodhouse, one and a half miles from Handsworth, but it lapsed for several years, and, on its revival, was transferred to the latter place. It is still danced at Christmas-time every year by colliers living in and about Handsworth, and it is certainly one of the best and most inspiriting of the dances that still survive in Yorkshire.

The team consists of eight dancers, two clowns, and a musician.

COSTUME.

Each dancer wears a tightly-fitting soldier's tunic of black velvet, with seven rays of white braid across the chest, narrowing in length to the waist, and cuffs of dark crimson velvet, the upper and lower edges of which are bound with white braid ; white ducks ; black leathern gaiters up to the knee ; stout black boots ; and a crimson velvet skull cap, shaped like a glengarry bonnet, with six coloured ribbons attached to the back, and two large pads of white and blue crocheted wool stitched to the front (*see* Frontispiece). The captain or leader (No. 1) wears a rosette on his left breast.

Each dancer carries a highly-polished sword, the blade of which is twenty-six inches long by one and a-half broad, fitted with a stout wooden hilt, five inches in length.

The two clowns are dressed like those in the modern circus.

THE MUSIC.

This is supplied by a concertina. Three tunes are used in the dance —" Napoleon's March," which is played in the first two figures only (the Ring and the Clash), either " The girl I left behind me " or " The White Cockade " for the next eight figures, and " The Keel Row " for the Roll.

The music controls the steps throughout the dance, while a prescribed number of bars is allotted to each figure in accordance with the directions presently to be given.

THE STEP.

This is a high-springing, exuberant, running step, the dancers as they bound from one foot to the other freely raising the knee of the free leg. In movements like the Ring, and whenever the dancer has a clear space before him, the step is executed as vigorously as possible. At other and less favourable moments in the dance, it is modified and danced more quietly. Occasionally, too, the dancers do a kind of shuffling step, lazily dragging the free leg on the ground. Before the beginning of the Roll the dancers use the heel-and-toe step described in the instructions.

THE DANCE.

Except for a slight pause, made between the Lock and the Roll, the following figures are performed in one continuous movement.

Figure 1.—The Ring.

The dancers shoulder their swords and stand in an arc, facing counter-clockwise, leaving a gap of three or four yards opposite the audience, between Nos. 1 and 2, thus:—

Bottom.

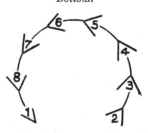

Top.

Audience.

They wait in this position while the musician plays the first strain of " Napoleon's March " (eight bars, A music), as in the Once-to-yourself of the Morris dance.

At the beginning of the second strain of the music (B) all dance round counter-clockwise, the leader and those immediately behind him quickly bridging, with three or four vigorous steps, the gap between them and No. 2 (eight bars, B music).

FIGURE 2.—THE CLASH.

All make a half-turn counter-clockwise and dance round clockwise, clashing their swords together in the usual way (eight bars A music, four bars B music, *twelve bars in all*). During the last four bars of B music the dancers link up, hilt-and-point, and dance round to a very vigorous step.

FIGURE 3.—THE SNAKE.

The leader, raising his left arm, jumps over his own sword. No. 2 then does the same, followed in order by Nos. 3, 4, 5, 6, 7, and 8 (eight bars, A music).

The leader, raising his right arm, then jumps over his left neighbour's sword, Nos. 8, 7, 6, 5, 4, 3, and 2, in turn, following suit (eight bars, B music).

FIGURE 4.—SINGLE-UP.

Bottom.

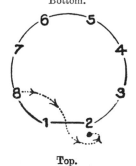

Top.

Audience.

No. 1, raising his sword and forming an arch with No. 2,
makes a whole turn clockwise, and faces him.   Simultaneously,
No. 8, raising his right arm, passes under the arch, turns to
his left, makes a half-turn counter-clockwise, faces No. 1,
and, standing by the side of No. 2, places his sword close to
and parallel with No. 1's sword.   Nos. 7, 6, 5, 4, and 3 now
pass under the two swords and turn to their left, while,
simultaneously, Nos. 8, 1, and 2 move down, keeping the two
raised swords close together and passing them over the heads
of the other five dancers.   Upon reaching the lower end,
No. 2, passing under No. 8's sword, moves forward to his
place between Nos. 1 and 3, turns clockwise, faces No. 3
and makes an arch with him (four bars).   The following
diagram shows the position when Nos. 8, 1, and 2, have
reached the lower end :—

Bottom.

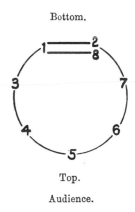

Top.

Audience.

Immediately No. 2 has raised his sword and made an arch
with No. 3, No. 1 passes under it (backward, if he pleases),
stands by the side of No. 3 and, raising his sword, places it
close to and parallel with No. 2's sword.   Nos. 2, 1, and 3
now move up to the top, hold the two swords close together
and pass them over the heads of Nos. 8, 7, 6, 5, and 4, all of

THE HANDSWORTH SWORD DANCERS.

SINGLE-UP. NO. 6 IS JUST PASSING UNDER THE SWORDS.

whom, on passing through the arch, turn to their left
as before (4 bars). The performers are now approximately
in their original positions.

These two movements, down and up, are repeated three
times, Nos. 3, 4, 5, 6, 7, and 8 successively raising their
swords. The figure occupies 32 bars in all.

Figure 5.—Single-Down.

No. 1 lowers his sword, over which Nos. 8, 7, 6, 5, 4, and 3,
in order, jump, turn to their left, and return to places (4 bars).

Directly No. 3 has passed over the sword, No. 2 leaps it,
turning counter-clockwise, and, as quickly as possible, lowers
his sword.

This movement is then repeated seven times, Nos. 2, 3, 4,
5, 6, 7, and 8 successively lowering their swords. The figure
occupies 32 bars in all.

Figure 6.—Double-Up.

The Handsworth men dance this figure in the same way as
Single-up (*see* p. 39), except that the two swords, which are
passed over the dancers, are held wide apart instead of
together. This method of execution is probably a corruption,
due to forgetfulness. It is suggested that the figure should
be performed in the following way:—

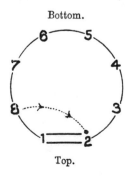

Bottom.

Top.

No. 1 forms an arch with No. 2. Simultaneously, No. 8 raises both hands, moves quickly forward, makes a half-turn counter-clockwise and faces No. 1, standing close at the right side of No. 2 and placing his sword parallel to No. 1's at a distance of about a yard from it. Nos. 7, 6, 5, 4, and 3, in order, then pass under the two swords and turn to their left round No. 2, while Nos. 1, 2, and 8 dance down to the bottom, holding the swords wide apart, and passing them over the heads of the other dancers. As they near the bottom No. 1 makes a whole turn clockwise; No. 8 passes quickly under No. 1's sword, turns to his left and passes round No. 2, who then moves forward to his place between Nos. 1 and 3 (4 bars).

No. 2 now forms an arch with No. 3. Simultaneously, No. 1 moves quickly forward and faces No. 2. The above movement is then repeated, Nos. 8, 7, 6, 5, and 4 passing under the two swords, while Nos. 2, 3 and 1 dance up to the top, holding the two swords wide apart and passing them over the heads of the other dancers. As they near the top No. 2 makes a whole turn clockwise; No. 1 passes quickly under No. 2's sword, turns to his left and passes round No. 3, who then moves forward to his place between Nos. 2 and 4 (4 bars).

These two movements, down and up, are then repeated three times, Nos. 3, 4, 5, 6, 7 and 8 successively raising their swords. The figure occupies 32 bars in all.

FIGURE 7.— DOUBLE-DOWN.

Bottom.

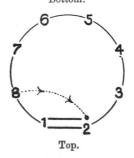

Top.

No. 1 lowers his sword and faces No. 2. Simultaneously, No. 8, raising his left arm, moves quickly toward No. 2, makes a half-turn clockwise, and, crouching at his right side, faces No. 1 and places his sword by the side of No. 1's sword. Nos. 7, 6, 5, 4, and 3 then in turn leap over the two swords, turn to their left and return to places. During this operation, No. 8 slowly creeps over the two swords, turns round No. 2 and, at the conclusion of the movement dances backward to his place. Directly No. 3 has leaped the swords, No. 2 does the same, making a whole-turn counter-clockwise; while No. 1, raising both arms, makes a whole turn counter-clockwise (4 bars). This movement is then repeated seven times, Nos. 2, 3, 4, 5, 6, 7, and 8 in turn lowering their swords. The figure occupies 32 bars in all. In each repetition the dancer who lowers the second sword must do so with the utmost speed and smartness, in order that the dancers behind him may leap over the two swords without delay.

FIGURE 8.—THREE-DIVIDE-UP.

Bottom.

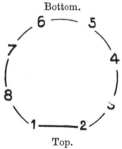

Top.

No. 1, raising both arms, makes a whole turn, clockwise, faces No. 2, and makes an arch with him. Nos. 8, 7, 6, 5, 4, and 3 immediately pass under the arch, Nos. 8, 7, and 6 turning to their left, Nos. 5, 4, and 3 to their right; while, simultaneously, Nos. 1 and 2 (together with No. 8, who stands close beside No. 2, holding his sword parallel to No. 1's, as in Single-up) move down to the lower end.

No. 2 now moves up till he faces No. 3, passing under the swords of Nos. 8 and 5. He then makes a half-turn, counterclockwise, and again moves down to the bottom, passing outside Nos. 6, 7, and 8, he and No. 3 raising the sword between them (No. 2's), under which the other dancers move up to places, dancing backward (8 bars).

This completes the first round; the dancers are now in the following positions, Nos. 2 and 3 still holding up the sword between them :—

Bottom.

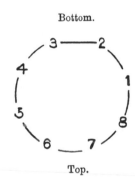

Top.

No. 2 now makes a whole turn clockwise. Nos. 1, 8, 7, 6, 5, and 4 then pass under the arch, Nos. 1, 8, and 7 turning to their left, Nos. 6, 5, and 4 to their right; while, simultaneously, Nos. 2 and 3 move up to the top. No. 3 then moves down till he faces No. 4 (passing under the swords of Nos. 1 and 6), turns counter-clockwise and dances up, he and No. 4 raising the sword between them (No. 3's), under which the rest of the dancers move down, dancing backward (8 bars).

This dual movement is then repeated three times, Nos. 3, 4, 5, 6, 7, and 8 successively raising their swords. The whole figure occupies 64 bars.

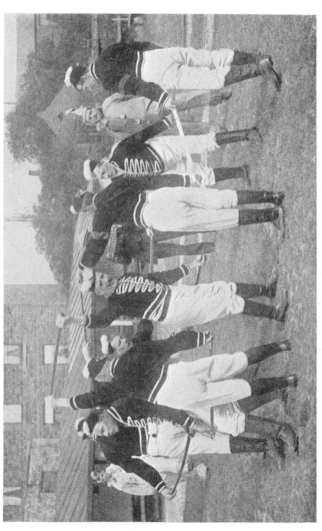

THE HANDSWORTH SWORD DANCERS.

THREE DIVIDE DOWN. NO. 3 HAS JUST JUMPED OVER THE SWORD.
NO. 2 WILL MAKE HIS COUNTER-CLOCK TURN THE NEXT MOMENT.

Figure 9.—Three-Divide-Down.

Bottom.

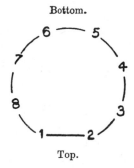

Top.

No. 1 lowers his sword, over which Nos. 8, 7, 6, 5, 4, and 3 in turn leap, Nos. 8, 7, and 6 turning to their left round No. 2, Nos. 5, 4, and 3 to their right round No. 1. Directly No. 3 has leaped the sword, No. 2 jumps over it, makes a three-quarter turn counter-clockwise, faces No. 3 and, together with him, dances down to the bottom, passing his sword over the heads of all the other dancers who move up to places under it, dancing backwards (eight bars), giving:—

Bottom.

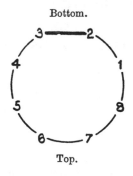

Top.

Nos. 2 and 3, upon reaching the bottom, immediately lower the sword between them, over which Nos. 1, 8, 7, 6, 5 and 4, in order, leap, Nos. 1, 8, and 7 turning to their left round No. 3, Nos. 6, 5, and 4 turning to their right round No. 2. Directly No. 4 has jumped over the sword, No. 3 leaps it, makes a three-quarter turn counter-clockwise, faces No. 4 and, together with him, dances up to the top, passing his sword over the heads of the other dancers who move down to places under it, dancing backwards (eight bars), giving:—

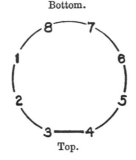

Bottom.

Top.

This dual movement is then repeated three times, down and up, Nos. 3, 4, 5, 6, 7, and 8 successively lowering their swords. The figure occupies 64 bars in all.

FIGURE 10.—THE LOCK.

All now dance round, clockwise, hilt-and-point, raising their feet and stamping them as loudly as possible (eight bars), regulating their pace so that at the end of the strain Nos. 1 and 2 have their backs to the audience. At the beginning of the next strain all make a whole turn counter-clockwise, face centre, close in, separate hands and lock the swords together, hilt over point.

One of the clowns then enters the ring, the Lock is placed round his neck, Nos. 1 and 2 move a step or two backward, and all face the audience, standing in the position shown in the diagram to the Ring (*see* p. 38). In the absence of the clowns, No. 8, directly the Lock is made, moves into the centre of the ring and is encircled with the swords.

Figure 11.—The Roll.

After a short pause the dancers place their swords on their right shoulders and stand in two files, facing one another thus:—

Bottom.

6>   <5

Right file.   7>   <4   Left file.

8>   <3

1>   <2

Top.

Standing in this position they dance the following heel-and-toe step for eight bars:—

T means a slight spring on to the toe, or ball of the foot, which takes the weight of the body.

H means a tap of the heel.

At the beginning of the next strain all lower their swords to a horizontal position, grasp the tips of their partners' swords with left hands and spin twice, the left-file dancer of the first and third couples once clockwise and once counter-clockwise, the right-file dancer of these couples once counter-clockwise and once clockwise; while the dancers of the second and fourth couples reverse the direction.

They then dance the Roll in the following way, all beginning simultaneously.

Each couple, going down from the top to the bottom, passes successively over, under, and over the three couples coming up; while each couple coming up from the bottom to the top passes successively under, over, and under the three couples going down.

After each change of position, every couple spins once — left-file dancers counter-clockwise, and right-file dancers clockwise, in going down; left-file dancers clockwise and right-file dancers counter-clockwise, in coming up.

Upon reaching either end and completing the change, *i.e.*, a pass *and a spin*, a couple spins twice, the first time in the direction it has previously been spinning, and the second time in the reverse direction (sometimes, neutral couples, instead of spinning, "step" in the way above described).

Each change—*i.e.*, a pass and a spin, or, in the case of neutral couples, two spins—occupies four bars of the music.

This movement is continued until all have returned to their original places (32 bars), and may be repeated as often as the leader pleases.

This brings the dance to a conclusion.

NOTATION.

THE AMPLEFORTH SWORD DANCE.

AMPLEFORTH is about eighteen miles due north of York. A sword-dance used to be performed there annually at Christmas-time until about twenty years ago, when it was discontinued. The following particulars have been acquired from one of the surviving dancers, Mr. George Wright, an ex-railwayman, seventy - five years of age, now living at Darlington. Mr. Wright, besides dancing, used on occasion to play the part of the Clown.

Although the dance itself is a good one and possesses many unusual features, the chief interest lies in the dramatic dialogue, the Folk-play, of which that dance is the central incident. For the purpose of this book it has been found necessary to omit several lines that were corrupt and unintelligible, and to amend others. It is hoped, however, that it will be found possible to print elsewhere the whole of the text exactly as Mr. Wright gave it me.

The company consisted of six dancers (of whom the leader was known as the King), a Clown, a Queen, a man to carry the flag inscribed " God save the Queen," two " beggars " with collecting tins, and two musicians.

COSTUME.

The dancers wore red soldier-tunics with rows of buttons from each shoulder converging toward the waist ; white trousers, with a red stripe down each leg ; and small blue military caps.

Each dancer carried a steel sword, the blade of which was twenty-nine inches long by one inch wide at the hilt, tapering to a quarter-inch at the point, with two notches immediately below the hilt, and a T-shaped projection at the tip. The hilt was of wood, five inches long.

The Clown wore a loose blue tunic extending below the waist, with red sleeves; white trousers; and a billycock hat with a bunch of coloured rags and a small bell attached to the back.

The Queen, impersonated by a man, was neatly dressed in bonnet and skirt and " hadn't had his hair cut for eighteen months, so it was frizzy and long."

THE PROCESSION.

When going from place to place the troupe marched in procession, thus : The two musicians, flag-bearer, Clown and Queen, the King and the rest of the dancers in couples.

THE MUSIC.

The music was performed by a fiddler and a drummer. No special air was traditionally associated with the dance, though the favourite tune seems to have been " The girl I left behind me."

The music controls the steps only, except where otherwise directed in the instructions. It is continuous throughout the dance.

THE STEP.

In the Clash, the Lock, and the Rose, the dancers walk, or tramp, in time with the music. All the other figures are executed to a quiet running step similar to that used by the Kirkby Malzeard dancers (*see* Part I., p. 41).

THE PLAY.

Except when otherwise directed, the following dialogue is to be spoken. The four tunes to which reference is made below, are printed in " The Sword Dances of Northern England, Songs and Dance Airs," Book III. The singing should, of course, be unaccompanied.

First Part.

[*Enter King and Clown.*

King :　Make room, make room for these jovial lads
　　　　That are a-wooing bound ;
　　　　For I can handle a sword
　　　　With any man in town.
　　　　Last night I went to see
　　　　Miss Madam Molly ;
　　　　She was so fair and comely
　　　　And not adorned with pride ;
　　　　I am so deep in love with her
　　　　That I don't know how to bide.
　　　　To-night I went to see
　　　　Miss Susannah Parkin ;
　　　　She was so fine and gay,
　　　　But the dogs made such a barkin'
　　　　I forgot all I had to say.
　　　　So I pray thee, honest Christian,
　　　　What next must I say to her ?

Clown :　Thou must give her gallant speeches,
　　　　And honestly must woo her.

King :　Ay, man, her mother likes me well ; she has forty
　　　　　thousand pound of her own and she'll give it
　　　　　all to myself.

Clown :　I'll stand thy friend right jarvey,
　　　　I'll stand thy friend, my lad ;
　　　　I'll stand thy friend right jarvey,
　　　　And, see thee, my heart's full glad.

King :　And many a better thing she'll give us when we
　　　　　get wed.

Clown :　Come thy ways ; I'll a-want* thee we'll get her.

[*Enter Queen.*

---

* Warrant.

*(From here to the end of the First Part the
dialogue is sung to Tune No. 1.)*

Clown :	Madam, behold a lover ! You shall quickly see my son.
Queen :	Long time have I been waiting, Expecting Ben would come : Ben's grown a smart young fellow And his face I long to see.
Clown :	Here's one that doth me follow, And perhaps it may be he. O Ben, how dost thou do, my lad ? Thou'st welcome from the seas.
King :	Thank you, father, how do you do ? I am very well at ease.
Clown :	O Ben, come let me kiss thee, For with joy I'm fit to cry.
King :	O father, I had rather kiss That lady standing by.
Clown :	O Ben, come show thy breeding ; Give to her a gentle touch. She's got such a face to feed on, The seas could afford none such. She's a sweet and honest creature, And she's of a noble fame ; She's a sweet and modest creature, And Susannah is her name.
King :	Father, that's well remembered. Pray, how is Dick and Val ?
Clown :	Poor Dick, his life is ended ; He's gone and left his all. Did I not write last summer That pale death had closed his eyes ?
King :	It's as true as I'm a sinner ! I had forgotten quite.
Clown :	Then it's home I will retire, For fear I'll spoil your sport :

For while I'm standing by here,
Our Ben can't frame to court.
So, Madam, don't be cruel,
Since you're a charmer fair:
Spare him as a jewel,
For you'll like to be my heir.

[Exit Clown.

King :   Madam, my father has declared
You are to be my wife;
Or otherwise I am inclined
To lead a single life.
For when a man gets married
He's down like a galley slave.
Bachelors like sailors are
With the liberties they have.

Queen :   O, Sir, who does compel you
Against your will to wed ?
Indeed, I needs must tell you,
You're but a loggers-head.*
Your cheek is none so charming
As to kindle Cupid's fire ;
You've neither wit nor larning,
Nor beauty to admire.

King :   *[Goes up to the Queen]* O, Madam, do but hear me !
I've got something more to say.

Queen :   *[Gives him a "pick."†]* Don't stand so near hand
by‡ me ;
Stand further off, I pray ;
I have not lost my hearing,
Nor yet I am not dumb !
But, in spite of all your jeering,
I can exercise my tongue.

---

* *i.e.*, Fool.   † Push.   ‡ Close to.

King :   Says thee so, thou Mistress Cheesemouth ?
           Thee might give me better words,
           Although thou 's a genteel carcase,
           Thy face it is absurd.
           Thy cheeks are cakes of tallow,
           Thy lips are blue all o'er ;
           Thou 's tawny black and yellow,
           And forty colours more !

> [*Queen goes up to the King again.   She
> gives him a " pick," and stamps her foot.*

Queen :   Begone ! thou piece of valour,
           For thou stinks of pitch and tar.
           Go hang thyself on the mainmast,
           Where I never shall see thee more.
           Take along with thee my wishes
           To the bottom of the sea ;
           Thou 's fitter for the fishes,
           Than a woman's company.

> [*Exeunt King and Queen.*

SECOND PART.

Clown :   Here comes I, that never come yet,
           With my great head and little wit.
           Though my head be great
           And my wit be small,
           I've six fine lads
           'll please you all.
           My head 's made of iron,
           My heart 's made of steel,
           My hands and feet of knuckle bone,
           I challenge thee out to feel !

> [*Enter King.   King and Clown cross swords
> and fight.*

King :   How long will this unthinking fool
           Disturb us of our privacy ?
           Fair Rose, thou may with boldness come
           And banish him from our company.
                              [Enter Queen.

Queen :   That would betray great want of skill ;
           It 's good to keep two strings for one bow.
           Perhaps I might bear him goodwill,
           As much as I might do to you !

Clown :   O, that 's well answered, my dear Rose,
           I love the girl that 's plain and free.
           Thou may be packing, snotty nose !
           Small hopes I find there is for thee.

King :   Surely this woman 's worse than mad !
           Judge, gentlemen, as well as me !
           In taking such a snotty lad,
           And despising such a spark as me !
                    [Straightens himself up.

Queen :   My father calls : I must obey.
           Be sure you both in peace remain,
           Till you hear further what I say
           The next time that we meet again.
                            [Exit Queen.

King :   Thou art a fool, O then say I,
           My reasons are expounded clean ;
           For women may riddle, but none can tell
           By plain subtraction what they mean.

Clown :   Still greater fool by half than I !
           Of what thou hears a woman say
           If thou would know the certainty,
           It 's meant quite the contráry way.
                             [Exit King.

Clown :   The devil go with them, for now they're gone and
           left me here behind ; I'll go and see if all 's
           well at home.   Faith man ! and I'll away
           an' all.
                            [Exit Clown.

THIRD PART.

King :   I'm a King and a Conqueror too,
And here I do advance !

Clown ·   I'm the clown of this noble town,
And I've come to see thee dance.

King :   The clown come to see a King dance !

Clown : A King dance ! I ask thee, good fellow, didn't I
see thee tending swine t'other day ?— stealing
swine, I meant to say.

King :   Now you've given offence to my Majesty. Thou
must either sing a song, or off goes your
head !

       [*The King tries to knock him about with his sword.*

Clown : I only know a lame song.

King :   I like a lame song.

Clown : How can I be merry and wise,
Or in my heart contented be ?
When the bone of my arm is out of place,
And he mun put his nose where the bone should be.

       [*Points his elbow at the King.*

King :   I ! Put my nose where the bone should be !
You old fool ! sing it over again, and sing it right.

Clown : I'll nobbut sing it again.

       [*Clown sings song as before but points his
elbow at another man.*

King :   As you've sung that so well, you must sing us
another.

Clown : How can I sing another when I don't know one ?

King :   I must have one, or off goes your head.

Clown : Let me study a minute. I've studied a love song
about murder my grandmother learned me
seven years after she was dead.

King :   O, I like a love song.

Clown:	O love, it is a killing thing,
	It's both for heart and mind ;
	And he that doesn't come before
	He needs must come befoor.
King:	You old fool, what difference is there between before and befoor ? Sing it over again, and sing it right.
Clown :	I'll nobbut sing it again.
King:	Sing it over again, and sing it right, or off goes your head !
Clown:	O love, it is a killing thing,
	It's both for heart and mind ;
	And he that doesn't come befoor,
	He needs must come before.
King:	What difference is there between befoor and before ? Sing it again and sing it right.
Clown:	It's the way I learned it.　 Sing it yourself.
King:	If I sing it, see that you learn it.
	O love, it is a killing thing,
	It's both for heart and mind ;
	And he that doesn't come before,
	He needs must come behind.

[King and Clown exeunt.

FOURTH PART.

[Enter King.

King:	I'm a king, and a king of high renown ;
	I'm sorry that I should be offended
	With that ragly fellow that's called a clown.

[Enter Clown.

Clown:	What needs thou be offended at me ?
	And make that great, long, ugly face at me ?
	If thou was hanged in yonder tree,
	I could make a far better king than thee !

King :   *[Goes up to dancers, who are behind the door.*

Come all ye young men, and draw your swords straight,

And take this fool clean out of my sight,

For if I talk to him, he'll talk to me all night.

        [Dancers rattle their swords. Exit King.

        (Sung to Tune No. 2.)

Clown : Ye gentlemen all, who in mirth take delight,

And intend our sport for to see,

I've come for to tell you that I am the Clown,

And, pray you, how do you like me ? *(bis).*

Although I am little, my strength it is great :

I would scorn for to tell you a lie,

I once killed a hedgehog as big as myself,

And it made me a rare apple-pie *(bis).*

My father was topsman and tidesman three years,

Alas ! he was til-ed so high :

It was all for stealing three lusty grey mares,

If that isn't true, it's a lie *(bis).*

Now as for myself, I'm a butcher so good,

I can hit both the mark and the square ;

I can stick a young heifer and never draw blood,

And that I can do to a hair *(bis).*

I always was jovial, and always will be,

Always at one time of the year,

Since Adam created both oxen and plough,

We get plenty of store and strong beer *(bis).*

        (Change to Tune No. 3.)

So now I've told my birth,

And the place from whence I come ;

So now I will set forth

Our noble dancers on.

Our dancers will appear

In splendour by and bye.

Gooks bobs ! I do them hear !

        [Dancers rattle their swords, but

        keep out of sight.

Silence ! Silence ! I cry.
Our dancers will appear
In splendour, red and white,
Gooks bobs ! and do them see,
They're coming into sight.

> [*The King just shows himself.*
> (*Change to Tune No.* 2.)

The first that comes on is King Henry by name,
He 's a King and a conqueror too ;
And with his broad sword he will make them
　　to fall ;
But I fear he will fight me, I vow　(*bis*).

> [*King enters and fights with Clown.*
> [*Enter No.* 2.

The next is Progallus, as some do him call,
He 's a general to the same king ;
And with his broad sword he will make them to fly ;
Isn't that a most desperate thing ?　(*bis*).

> [*Enter No.* 3.

The third I shall name without any offence,
He 's a gentleman just come from Cork ;
He 's witty, he 's pretty in every degree,
And amongst the girls he will sport　(*bis*).

> [*Enter No.* 4.

The fourth it is Hickman, a rival of mine,
And a passionate lover is he ;
He 's always bewitched by a beautiful lass,
But young Cupid his ruin shall be　(*bis*).

> [*Enter No.* 5.

The fifth it is Jerry, a passionate friend,
He follows his master indeed ;
He 's been a true trudger as ever did bend,
And I wish we'd some more of his breed　(*bis*).

> [*Enter No.* 6.

Here's little Diana I'd like to forgot,
Whose beauty shines much like my own ;
But if ever we get our heads to the pot
We'll drink till't strikes fourteen at noon　(*bis*).

　　　　　　　　[*The six dancers exeunt.*
　　　　　　　　(*Change to Tune No.* 1.)

Go on, my six brave heroes ;
Our valour has been tried ;
All on the plains of Waterloo
These six fought side by side.
They fought against Napoleon bold,
And made him run away ;
They sent him to St. Helena,
And there they made him stay.
Now all you pretty lasses,
That's sitting round about,
These are six handsome young lads
As ever was turned out.
They'll make you loving sweethearts,
For ever they'll be true ;
They'll fight for you as manfully
As they did at Waterloo.

　　　　　　[*Enter No.* 1, *the King.　He walks round*
　　　　　　　　in a small circle, clockwise, with his
　　　　　　　　sword over his shoulder.　The other
　　　　　　　　dancers, as they enter, walk behind him,
　　　　　　　　in order.

The first that I do call upon
He is a noble king ;
He is as handsome a young man
As ever the sun shone on.
He's like his brother Cupid :
Look on the charming boy !
And when he meets with a bonny lass
With her he loves to toy.

　　　　　　　　　　[*Enter No.* 2.

The next he is a bashful youth,
He 's brother to the moon ;
But doesn't he get his name up
In country and in town.
Amongst the pretty wenches
He drives a roaring trade ;
And when he meets with a bonny lass
His valour is displayed.

> [*Enter No.* 3.

The next he is a sparkly lad,
With his broad sword in his hand ;
He'll show you honest sword-play
As any in the land.
So now I bid thee come thy way
All with thy valiant spear,
For thou canst act a gallant part
As well as any here.

> [*Enter No.* 4.

The next he is a rakish youth ;
I've heard his mother say
That she'd give him some good advice
Before he went away.
He was never to kiss a black lass
When he could kiss a white,
But when he met with a bonny lass
To kiss her, black or white !

> [*Enter No.* 5.

The next he is a valiant youth,
All in the wars he 's been ;
When he returned from Waterloo,
The bells did loudly ring.
He won the day in splendour,
He fought a valiant main.
His countrymen did all rejoice
When he returned again.

> [*Enter No.* 6.

The next he is as brave a man
As any you did see ;
So well he did act his part
For his King and count-e-ry.
He's got no fear about him :
For ever he'll be true ;
He'll fight for you as manfully
As he fought at Waterloo.

(*Change to Tune No. 3.*)

So lasses prepare your lips
Or else before your eyes
These six lusty lads I've got
Will carry off the prize.
So speak, spectators all,
If you'll not take it amiss,
While these lads dance their shares,
These lasses I will kiss.
So now you've seen us all,
Think of us what you will ;
Music ! strike up and play
" T'aud wife of Coverdill."

[*The musician strikes up, and the dancers
at once execute the following figures.*

THE DANCE.

The Clash.

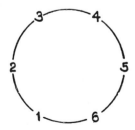

The dancers, in the above order, walk round, clockwise clashing their swords in the usual way (4 bars), and there making a half-turn clockwise, march back to places, clashing as before (4 bars).

The Ring.

They then dance round in a ring, clockwise, each man placing his sword over his right shoulder and grasping the tip of the sword in front of him (4 bars). All now raise right hands, place their swords on left shoulders, and continue dancing round clockwise (4 bars), so regulating their pace that at the end of the movement Nos. 1 and 6 have their backs to the audience.

Fourth-Man-Over.

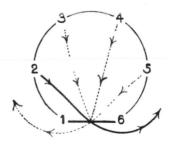

No. 1 lowers his sword, over which Nos. 5, 4, 3, and 2 successively jump and return to places, Nos. 5, 4, and 3 turning to their right round No. 1, No. 2 to his left round No. 6. Immediately No. 2 has jumped the sword No. 6, raising his right arm, leaps the sword and makes a whole turn counter-clockwise; while No. 1 stands up and with his left arm guides No. 2 to his place.

This movement is then repeated five times, Nos. 2, 3, 4, 5, and 6 successively lowering their swords.

Fourth-Man-Under.

No. 1 raises his sword and forms an arch with No. 6. Nos. 5, 4, 3, and 2 then pass under the raised sword and return to places, Nos. 5, 4, and 3 turning to their right round No. 1, No. 2 to his left round No. 6.

Directly No. 2 has passed under the arch, No. 1 makes a whole turn, clockwise, and, with his left arm, guides No. 2 to his place ; while No. 6 makes a whole turn counter clockwise.

This movement is then repeated five times, Nos. 2, 3, 4, 5, and 6 in turn raising their swords and making an arch.

Third-Man-Over.

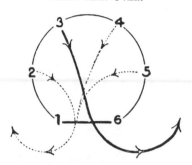

No. 1 lowers his sword, over which Nos. 5, 4, 3, and 2 successively leap and return to places, Nos. 5, 4 and 2 turning to their right round No. 1, No. 3 to his left round No. 6. As No. 2 leaps the sword, No. 1 passes his left arm over his head. No. 6 then raising his right arm, jumps over the sword and turns counter-clockwise.

This movement is then repeated five times, Nos. 2, 3, 4, 5, and 6 successively lowering their swords.

Third-Man-Under.

No. 1 raises his sword and makes an arch with No. 6. Nos. 5, 4, 3, and 2 then pass under the arch and return to places, Nos. 5, 4, and 2 turning to their right round No. 1,

No. 3 to his left round No. 6. Directly No. 2 has passed under the arch, No. 1 makes a whole turn clockwise, while No. 6 makes a whole turn counter-clockwise.

This movement is then repeated five times, Nos. 2, 3, 4, 5, and 6 successively raising their swords and making an arch.

DOUBLE-OVER.

This is performed in the same way as Double-over in the Kirkby Malzeard dance (*see* Part I., p. 50), except that Nos. 1, 2, 3, 4, 5, and 6 successively lower their swords, and that at the end of each round *both* dancers, who lower the sword, leap over it.

DOUBLE-UNDER.

This is performed in the same way as in the Kirkby Malzeard dance (*see* Part I., p. 49), Nos. 1, 2, 3, 4, 5, and 6 successively raising their swords and making an arch.

PLAITING.

The dancers now release the points of their left neighbours' swords, divide into couples, each man grasping the tip of his partner's sword and placing his own close beside it, and stand thus :—

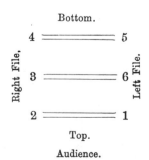

Bottom.

4 ══════ 5

Right File.

3 ══════ 6

Left File.

2 ══════ 1

Top.

Audience.

They then perform the following movements :—

(1) First and second couples change places, Nos. 1 and 3 moving four steps forward and four steps backward, alternately pushing and pulling their partners; while Nos. 4 and 5 spin twice, No. 4 clockwise, No. 5 counter-clockwise (4 bars).

(2) First and third couples change places, Nos. 1 and 4 moving four steps backward and four steps forward, alternately pulling and pushing their partners; while Nos. 3 and 6 spin twice, No. 3 clockwise, No. 6 counter-clockwise (4 bars).

(3) Second and third couples change places, Nos. 6 and 4 moving four steps forward and four steps backward, alternately pushing and pulling their partners; while Nos. 1 and 2 spin twice, No. 1 counter-clockwise, No. 2 clockwise (4 bars).

These changes are continued until the three couples are once again in their original places (6 changes, *i.e.*, 24 bars). The whole movement is then repeated as often as the leader pleases.

It will be seen that in starting to go up or down the dance the left-file dancer begins the first change by pushing his partner, and the second change by pulling him ; while neutral couples spin twice, left-file dancers counter-clockwise, right file clockwise.

Waves-of-the-Sea.

The dancers, still in couples, but holding their swords wider apart, stand as shown in the preceding diagram, and then dance the Roll as in the Sleights dance (*see* Part II., p. 25).

Three-Reel.

The dancers now divide into two sets of three, and stand, each set in hilt-and-point formation, thus:

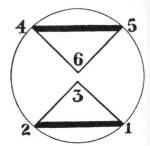

No. 2 raises his sword. No. 3 passes under, turns to his left round No. 1, making about three-quarters of a circuit; immediately No. 3 has passed under the arch, No. 2 moves counter - clockwise round No. 1 and No. 3, thus overtaking him. Simultaneously No. 1 makes a whole turn counter - clockwise. These movements are performed simultaneously by the other set of dancers, No. 5 corresponding to No. 2, No. 6 to No. 3 and No. 4 to No. 1, giving

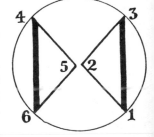

The evolution is repeated twice, Nos. 1 and 3 successively raising their swords in the one set, and Nos. 4 and 6 in the other set. Whilst these evolutions are being performed, the two sets of dancers move round each other counter-clockwise.

The above figures are repeated as many times as the leader may elect.

At a signal from the leader, all six form a ring in original order, face clockwise, place swords on right shoulders, grasp the tips of the swords in front, and dance round to the end of the strain.

The Ring.

As before (*see* p. 64).

Third-Man-Over.

As before (*see* p. 65). At the conclusion of the movement all dance round clockwise, hilt-and-point, to the end of the strain.

Nip-it Lock.

At the beginning of the next strain all raise their arms, make a whole turn, clockwise, lock the swords together, and then move slowly round till the end of the strain (8 bars).

The Wheel.

At the beginning of the next strain all walk round clockwise, while the leader, holding the Lock by his own hilt in his right hand, raises it above his head, arm erect. At the end of the first bar he passes it behind him to No. 6, who grasps it by his own hilt and, at the end of the second bar, passes it behind him to No. 5. In this way the Lock is passed round the ring until it returns to the leader, each dancer in turn receiving it from the man in front and passing it to the man behind. All then march round to the end of the strain (8 bars).

This movement may be lengthened by each dancer retaining the Lock for two or more bars instead of one, the movement in that case taking 16 bars or more instead of 8.

The Rose.

This is performed in one or other of two ways, according as the dance is performed with or without the Play.

When the dance only is done the figure is performed as follows: The leader places the Lock on the ground in the centre of the ring, and all dance round, clockwise (4 bars). The dancers then clap three times, on the two beats of the fifth bar and the first beat of the sixth; while the Clown, after throwing down his sword, claps three times on the second beat of the fifth bar and the two beats of the sixth. All now stoop down, raise the Lock to waist-level, each holding the hilt of his own sword in his right hand, and, on the second beat of the last bar, smartly draw their swords from the Lock.

When the dance is performed as an integral part of the Play, the Rose is executed as follows.

An outsider, in ordinary dress, enters the ring, and the Lock is placed round his neck. The dancers now walk round, clockwise, each holding his own hilt in his right hand (4 bars). In the fifth and sixth bars the Clown and the dancers each clap three times in the way described above. At the beginning of the seventh bar all dance round, clockwise, each holding the hilt of his own sword in his right hand, and, on the second beat of the last bar of the strain, draw their swords smartly from the Lock. The man in the ring at once falls to the ground and feigns death, while the dancers, terrified at what they have done, run away and hide themselves, leaving the Clown and the dead man alone on the stage.

NOTATION.

The Clash (*see* p. 63).
The Ring (*see* p. 64).
Fourth-Man-Over (*see* p. 64).
Fourth-Man-Under (*see* p. 65).
Third-Man-Over (*see* p. 65).
Third-Man-Under (*see* p. 65).
Double-Over (*see* p. 66).
Double-Under (*see* p. 66).
Plaiting (*see* p. 66).
Waves-of-the-Sea (*see* p. 67).
Three-Reel (*see* p. 68).
The Ring (*see* p. 64).
Third-Man-Over (*see* p. 65).
Nip-it Lock (*see* p. 69).
The Wheel (*see* p. 69).
The Rose (*see* p. 69).

Fifth Part.

[*The Clown walks about with his head in the
air and tumbles over the corpse.*

Clown: It's rough ground!

[*He turns round, walks backward, and
tumbles over again.*

[*Enter King.*

King: Hullo! hullo! what's the matter here?

Clown: A man dead.

King: I fear you've killed him.

Clown: No! He's very near killed me! (*Stamps his feet.*)
Come, all you villains, and clear yourselves.

[*Enter No. 2.*

No. 2
(*spoken*): I am sure it's none of I
That did this bloody act;
It's he that follows me
That did it, for a fact.

[*Enter No. 3.*

No. 3: I'm sure it's none of I
That did this awful crime;
It's he that follows me
That drew his sword so fine.

[*Enter No. 4.*

No. 4: Don't lay the blame on me,
You awful villains all;
I'm sure my eyes were shut
When this young man did fall.

[*Enter No. 5.*

No. 5: How could your eyes be shut
When I was looking on?
I'm sure that you were with us
When first our swords were drawn.

[*Enter No 6.*

No. 6 :   Our King has done the deed,
And he lays the blame on me.
Before I'll take the blame
I'll try my sword with thee.

> [*The King and No.* 6 *cross swords and fight.*

King :   Oray! Alas! what shall I do?
I've been the cause of all this war.
Oray I am that it should happen so,
That I should slay this poor old man.

Clown :   How can he be an old man? A young man
like me, his father! I got * him this morning
before I got my breakfast. Bury him! We'll
sing a psalm over him.

> [*All kneel round the dead man. The Clown
> stands up and gives out the following
> lines in a stentorian voice, the dancers
> repeating each couplet after the Clown.
> and singing the lines to Tune No.* 4.

Clown :   When first King Henry ruled this land
He was a right generous king ;

He stole three pecks of barley-meal
To make a large pudding.

And when this pudding it was boiled,
They filled it full of plums,

And there was lumps of suet in
As big as my two thumbs.

> [*Each singer puts his two thumbs together
> and holds them up.*

The King and Queen they both did eat,
And gentlemen likewise ;

---

* Begot.

And what they couldn't eat that night
Next morning had it fried.

> [*The Clown now reads the dead man's Will.
> He hands his sword to a bystander and
> then produces a dirty piece of paper out
> of his pocket.*

Clown :   Tom and Jerry up a tree. . . . . . .
(Sings)

King :   No! That's wrong. Read it right.

Clown :   God in heaven take my soul;
(Reads)   Churchyard take my bones :
And that man, that holds my sword,
Take my wife and bairns.

King :   How can we
This man burie,
When people all around us stand ?
But if we mean to escape a halter,
For a doctor we must send.

> [*All shout for a doctor.*

King :   I have heard of doctors, far and near ;
I have heard of one, though he lives in Spain ;
I'll lay ten pounds, if he was here,
He would bring this man to life again.
Five, ten, fifteen, twenty pounds for a doctor !

> [*Enter Doctor, riding on the back of another
> man. He dismounts.*

Doctor :   See, Sir, a doctor here, who travels much at home.
Take these here, my pills! They cure the
young, the old, the hot, the cold, the living
and the dead. What the devil's the matter
here ?

King :   A man dead.

Doctor :   How long has he been dead ?

King :   Seven minutes. Can you cure him ?

Doctor :   If he has been dead seven years, I can cure him.

King : What is your fee ?

Doctor : My fee is nineteen pounds, nineteen shillings, eleven-pence three farthings, a peck of gingerbread, and some oats for my horse.

King : It is an imposition ! I shan't pay it.

Doctor : Gee, Ball ! (*mounts and rides off*).

King : Hi! Hi! Doctor! Is that the lowest you will take ?

[*Enter Doctor.*

Doctor : I'll throw off the oats and the gingerbread.

King : You must try your skill.

[*The Doctor kneels down and feels the dead man's pulse.*

Doctor : He has got a raging pulse !

Clown : How can a dead man have a raging pulse ?

[*The Doctor pretends to give him a pill. The Clown pulls him away.*

Clown : Giving a dead man physic ?

King : Can you cause a stomach* in the morning ?

Doctor : I can cause a stomach in the morning, make his victuals fly down his throat like a two-legged wheelbarrow, and rattle in his bowels like a pair of chests of drawers.

King : Can you do anything for a fair lady ?

Doctor : Yes! If ever a fair lady in this room wants a husband, bring her to me, and I'll find her one.
Of thousands which I've cured,
There's no one here can tell.
It's all this little vandorious† box. (*Taps box.*)
Take this, take that, and you're well.

King : Well, doctor, what is your name ?

Doctor : I don't like to tell it to a ragamuffin like you.

King : I must know your name.

---

* Appetite.   † Pandora's.

Doctor : Well, you shall know it, but it takes a good scholar to read it.   My name is Ivan-lovan-tantaman, laddie, seventh son of a new-born doctor. Here I've travelled through fifty-five kingdoms and now return to my own again ; cure men with their heads off, men with their hearts out, the itch, the stitch, the stone, the bone, the pulse, and the gout ; and if there are nineteen devils in a man I can fetch twenty out.

King : Hi ! Doctor, he's a long time coming to life !

Doctor : Well, I must bleed him.

> [*Whereupon the Clown sharpens first the hilt and then the point of his sword, and gives the King the dead man's arm to hold up. He then backs a few paces, and runs at the arm with his sword. This he misses, but hits the King instead, who, crying out* " Ten thousand murthers !" *tumbles down and knocks off his knee-cap. This however, the Doctor puts right. The Clown then helps to bleed the dead man in the wrist, which he ties up in a handkerchief.*

Doctor : I've travelled for my education.

King : How far have you travelled ?

Doctor : All the way from the fireside, upstairs, knocked the looking-glass over, and back again.

King : Is that all you have travelled ?

Doctor : Oh, no ! not by a great deal. I've travelled all the way from Itti-Titti, where there's neither town nor city, wooden churches, leather bells, black puddings for bell-ropes, little pigs running up and down the street with knives and forks stuck in their backs, crying " God save the Queen ! "

King :   Well, doctor, he is a long time coming to life

Clown :   I'll fetch him back to life.

> [*The Clown moves the dead man's feet to
> one side, and then, when the King
> says that that is wrong, moves them
> to the other. The King saying that
> this is also wrong, the Clown stretches
> the legs apart and putting his sword
> to the dead man's throat, draws it
> down the middle of his body. At this
> the dead man comes to life, jumps up
> and sings the following lines to tune
> No. 3 :—*

Good morning, gentlemen,
A-sleeping I have been ;
I've had such a sleep
As the like was never seen.
And now I am awake
And alive unto this day,
Our dancers shall have a dance,
And the doctor have his pay.

> [*The dancers then form up, and perform a
> figure or two of their dance. This
> concludes the entertainment.*

THE ASKHAM RICHARD SWORD DANCE.

At Askham Richard, about five miles south-west of York, a sword dance used annually to be performed for a week—or sometimes two weeks—after Christmas. The custom was discontinued about forty years ago.

The company consisted of eight dancers, a Fool, a Besom-Betty, a King, a Queen, two men carrying a large banner suspended between two poles and bearing the legend, " God speed the plough," three musicians, and two " beggars " with small collecting tins.

COSTUME.

The dancers were dressed in white calico tunics extending below the waist, and trimmed with red braid ; white ducks, with a red stripe down each leg ; and high hats covered with ribbons when they walked in procession ; or wire wreaths of artificial flowers when they danced.

Each dancer carried a wooden sword of ash, about three feet long, pointed at one end and thickened at the handle-end by the addition of two blocks of wood fastened on either side. In the procession, small coloured flags were attached to the tips of the swords. These were square, about the size of a small pocket-handkerchief, with a broad hem, or slot, so as to slip on or off as required. The Fool carried a long stick, or pole, with a bladder tied to one end.

The Besom-Betty, impersonated by a man, was dressed in an old frock and scuttle-bonnet, and carried a broom to sweep away the snow and clear a place for the dancers (" We used to enjoy ourselves proper, but it wanted to be frost and snaw," my informant remarked).

THE MUSIC.

This was supplied by two fiddlers and a drummer. During the procession any suitable slow march tune was played. For the dance, " The Fisher Laddie " was the usual tune—sometimes varied, however, by a curious air consisting of a combination of " The girl I left behind me " and " The British Grenadiers."

Ordinarily, the music controls the steps only ; but, as will be seen later on, certain figures begin or end synchronously with one or other of the strains of the music.

Except between the figures, where a slight pause is made, the music is played continuously throughout the dance.

The musician must be careful to begin the Rose with the first strain, A, of the music.

THE STEP.

This is a springy, running step like that used in the Kirkby Malzeard Dance, but rather more lively (*see* Part I., p. 41). This step is continued throughout the dance, except in the Clash and the Rose, where a modified and quieter form of it is used.

THE PROCESSION.

When moving from place to place the company marched in procession in the following order : The two banner-bearers ; the King and Queen, arm-in-arm ; the Besom-Betty and the Fool, arm-in-arm ; the eight dancers in single file, waving their flags above their heads. All marched along slowly in the above order except the dancers, who executed a straight hey as they advanced in the following manner. The hindmost dancer, quickening his pace, passed to the right of the second dancer, to the left of the third, and in this manner threaded his way to the top of the column, where he slowed down and marched behind the Besom-Betty and the Fool. Directly the hindmost man had passed the third dancer, the second man heyed to the top of the column in like manner. This movement was continued in turn by the rest of the dancers throughout the march, each successively heying from the bottom of the column to the top, and then marching along slowly until the remaining seven dancers had passed him, when he once again repeated the process.

On arriving at its destination, the procession broke up; the dancers exchanged their high hats for the flower-wreaths, removed the flags from their swords, and lined up in the following order:

8	7	6	5	4	3	2	1
V	V	V	V	V	V	V	V

Audience.

The Fool then sang a song (unfortunately forgotten), in which he called out the dancers in order, one by one, while he walked slowly round in a ring, clockwise, between the audience and the dancers. Each man, on being called, left the file and walked behind the Fool.

At the conclusion of the song the Fool left the ring and faced the dancers, standing with his back to the audience. Here he was joined by the King, who, waving his sword, addressed the dancers in a loud voice—

> I am a king and a conqueror,
> And now do I advance!

To which the Fool added—

> And I am a clown, an ugly clown,
> And I've come to see you dance.

The King and the Fool now stepped aside, the former calling out "Now, my boys, present! Rattle up!" The dancers then proceeded to execute the following figures.

THE DANCE.

The movements in each of the following figures are continuous. A slight pause should be made between the figures.

FIGURE 1.

The Ring.

The dancers dance round in a ring, clockwise, waving their swords above their heads, hilts at chin-level, for eight bars (A music) in the following order :—

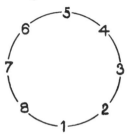

The Clash.

The dancers continue dancing round, clockwise, clashing their swords together in time with the music in the usual way (8 bars, B music). They then quickly make a half-turn, clockwise, and dance back to places, holding their swords in their right hands, and clashing as before (8 bars, A music).

Your-Own-Sword.

All face centre, linking up hilt-and-point. No. 1 then raises his left arm and leaps over his own sword, the rest of the dancers, in order, following suit. The dancers then dance round, clockwise, until the end of the strain (8 bars, B music). This movement is then repeated seven times, Nos. 2 3, 4, 5, 6, 7, and 8 in turn initiating the evolution.

Single-Over.

As in the Kirkby Malzeard dance (*see* Part I., p. 47), Nos. 1, 2, 3, 4, 5, 6, 7, and 8 successively lowering their swords.

SINGLE-UNDER.

As in the Kirkby Malzeard dance (*see* Part I., p. 45) Nos. 1, 2, 3, 4, 5, 6, 7, and 8 in turn raising their swords.

NIP-IT LOCK.

The dancers dance round, clockwise, hilt-and-point, till the end of the strain of the music. They then halt, face centre, and swing their arms forward and backward on the first and middle beats of the first bar of the next strain. At the beginning of the second bar, they swing their arms forward and over their heads, close in a little, make a whole-turn, clockwise, separate their hands and, moving slowly round clockwise, lock the swords together by bending hilts under points (8 bars).

THE ROSE.

The leader, No. 1, raising the Lock in his right hand, arm erect, moves into the centre of the ring and turns slowly round on his axis, counter-clockwise, while the rest of the dancers dance round, clockwise (8 bars, A music).

The leader then returns to his place in the ring and lowers the Lock to a horizontal position, waist-high. Each man grasps the hilt of his sword with his right hand and all dance round, clockwise, drawing their swords smartly from the Lock on the last note of the last bar of the music (8 bars, B music).

FIGURE 2.

THE CLASH.

As in Figure 1.

DOUBLE-OVER.

As at Kirkby Malzeard (*see* Part I., p. 50), except that three, instead of two, couples leap in turn over the lowered sword. The movement is performed eight times, Nos. 1, 2, 3, 4, 5, 6, 7, and 8 successively lowering their swords.

Double-Under.

This is done as in the Sleights dance (*see* Part II., p. 21), except that in each round three, instead of two, couples pass under the raised sword, and Nos. 1, 2, 3, 4, 5, 6, 7, and 8 in turn raise their swords.

Back Lock.

The dancers dance round, hilt-and-point, clockwise, till the end of the strain of the music.   The Back Lock is then performed as in the Sleights dance (*see* Part II., p. 22), except that the arms rest upon the shoulders of the performers instead of being placed behind the waists.

The Rose.

As in Figure 1 (*see* p. 81).

FIGURE 3.

The Clash.

As in Figure 1 (*see* p. 80).

Double-Sword-Down.

As in Double-Swords-Down (alternative version) of the Grenoside Dance (Part 1, p. 113) except that when the two swords have been lowered as there described, there remain *five* dancers to pass over and they do so in this order (for the first round) : Nos. 7, 6, 5, 4, and 3.   The movement is performed eight times, Nos. 1, 2, 3, 5, 6, 7 and 8 successively lowering their swords.

Double-Sword-Up.

As in the Grenoside Dance, alternative version (Part 1, p. 113) with the same qualifications *mutatis mutandis* as in the last figure.   This movement is done eight times, Nos. 1, 2, 3, 4, 5, 6, 7 and 8 successively raising their swords.

Shoulder Lock.

All move round, hilt-and-point, clockwise, until the beginning of the next strain of the music. They then leave go of the points of their neighbours' swords, face counter-clockwise round the ring (turning clockwise in order to do so), place their own swords over their right shoulders and grasp with their left hand the tips of the swords in front of them. In this formation they dance round, counter-clockwise, for a bar or so, until, at a word from the leader, all raise their arms above their heads, make a three-quarter turn clockwise, face centre, close in, separate hands, and lock the swords together, passing hilts over points. They then dance round, clockwise, until the end of the strain of the music (8 bars).

The Rose.

As in Figure 1 (*see* p. 81).

FIGURE 4.

The Clash.

As in Figure 1 (*see* p. 80).

The Roll.

The dancers now stand in pairs, each man grasping the tip of his partner's sword, in the following order :—

Bottom.

5 ═══════ 4

6 ═══════ 3

7 ═══════ 2

8 ═══════ 1

Top.

They then do the Roll as in the Handsworth dance (*see* p. 47), omitting the prefatory shuffle and double spin and starting the changes straight away. This movement is continued as long as the leader elects. The dancers then form a ring, in original order, hilt-and-point, and dance round clockwise till the end of the strain of the music.

THE RIDE LOCK.

Releasing the points of their neighbours' swords, all face counter-clockwise round the ring (turning clockwise as before), pass the points of their swords between their legs and, with left hands, grasp the points of the swords in front of them. After dancing round in this formation for a few bars, at a signal from the leader, all lift their left legs over their own swords, face centre, close in, separate hands, and lock the swords together, hilts above points.

THE ROSE.

As in Figure 1 (*see* p. 81). When, however, in B music, the Lock is lowered horizontally, the Fool creeps into the ring, kneels down in the centre, and passes his head under and through the middle of the Lock. When the swords are drawn from the Lock, the Fool tumbles down and feigns death. All cry " A doctor! a ten-pound doctor!" Whereupon, a doctor, in top-boots and with a bottle in his hand, comes upon the scene and attempts to revive the dead man. In this he fails. The Besom-Betty then comes to the rescue, and saying " A'll cure him!" brushes the face of the Fool with her broom. She is as good as her word; the Fool rises to his feet, rubs his eyes, and all ends happily. This concludes the dance.

NOTATION.

Figure 1.

> The Ring (*see* p. 80).
> The Clash (*see* p. 80).
> Your-own-sword (*see* p. 80).
> Single-over (*see* p. 80).
> Single-under (*see* p. 81).
> Nip-it Lock (*see* p. 81).
> The Rose (*see* p. 81).

Figure 2.

> The Clash (*see* p 80).
> Double-over (*see* p. 81).
> Double-under (*see* p. 82).
> Back Lock (*see* p. 82).
> The Rose (*see* p. 81).

Figure 3.

> The Clash (*see* p. 80).
> Double-sword-down (*see* p. 82).
> Double-sword-up (*see* p. 82).
> Shoulder Lock (*see* p. 83).
> The Rose (*see* p. 81).

Figure 4.

> The Clash (*see* p. 80).
> The Roll (*see* p. 83).
> The Ride Lock *see* p. 84).
> The Rose (*see* p. 84).

THE HAXBY SWORD DANCE.

HAXBY is a small village about three miles north of York. Although it is twenty-three years since the sword dance was performed there, four of the dancers are still living, and it is from these that the following particulars have been obtained. Haxby and the neighbouring village of Wigginton each supplied a complete team of dancers, both of which danced the same dance.

There were eight dancers, a Fool or Clown, a King, a Queen, a Besom-Betty, an accordion-player, and two collectors.

COSTUME.

Each dancer wore a white shirt covered, back and front, with small bows and rosettes of variously coloured ribbons; a white silk scarf, three inches wide, across the right shoulder, the ends hanging down over the left hip; black trousers with a red stripe down each leg; and a red cap. Each dancer carried a wooden sword of ash, three feet long by one-and-a-half inches wide, pointed at one end, with a cross piece, four inches long, below and at right angles to the hilt.

The other characters were dressed in the usual way, the Besom-Betty and Queen being, of course, impersonated by men.

THE MUSIC.

No special tune was traditionally associated with the dance, but the one most frequently used was "The girl I left behind me."

The opening figure, the Clash, is performed to the second strain (B) of the tune. As the last three figures are each performed in eight bars of the music, the musician must accompany the first of these, the Right-Shoulder Lock, with the second strain (B) of the air. The rest of the figures are danced independently of the music, which controls the steps only.

No pause whatever is made between any of the movements, the dance proceeding from beginning to end without break of any kind.

THE STEP.

In the Clash, the Right-Shoulder Lock, the Wheel, and the Rose the dancers walk or march; but throughout the rest of the dance they use the easy, springing, running-step described in the Kirkby Malzeard dance (*see* Part I., p. 41).

THE DANCE.

The dancers, swords over right shoulders, stand in a ring, facing clockwise, while the musician plays the first strain of the tune (8 bars), thus :—

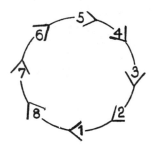

They then perform the following figures :—

FIGURE 1.— THE CLASH.

As in the Escrick dance (*see* p. 28).

FIGURE 2.—THE SNAKE.

As in the Handsworth dance (*see* p. 39).

Figure 3.—Single-Over.

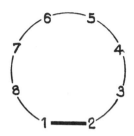

No. 1 lowers his sword, over which Nos. 8, 7, 6, 5, 4, and 3 in succession leap, turn to their right round No. 1, and dance back to places, each dancer passing behind those who have preceded him over the sword. As No. 8 jumps the sword, No. 1 passes his left hand over his head; and directly No. 3 has leaped over the sword No. 2 jumps over it, turning counter-clockwise, and, with a circular sweep of his right arm, guides No. 3 to his place, passing his sword over the heads of the other dancers.

This movement is then repeated seven times, Nos. 2, 3, 4, 5, 6, 7, and 8 successively lowering their swords.

Figure 4.—Single-Under.

No. 1 raises his sword and makes an arch with No. 2. Nos. 8, 7, 6, 5, 4, and 3 then pass in turn under the sword, turn to their right round No. 1, and dance back to their places, each passing behind those who have preceded him. As the dancers pass under the arch, No. 1 gradually makes a whole turn clockwise; and immediately No. 3 has passed under it, No. 2 quickly makes a whole turn counter-clockwise, and then, with a circular sweep of his right arm, guides No. 3 to his place, passing his sword over the heads of the other dancers.

This movement is then repeated seven times, Nos. 2, 3, 4, 5, 6, 7, and 8 in turn making an arch with their swords.

Figure 5.—Double-Over.

As in the Kirkby Malzeard dance (*see* Part I., p. 50), except that No. 1 lowers his sword in the first round, and Nos. 2, 3, 4, 5, 6, 7, and 8 in the seven succeeding ones.

Figure 6.—Double-Under.

This movement is the same as that of Double-under in the Sleights dance (*see* Part II., p. 21), except that No. 1 raises his sword in the first round, and Nos. 2, 3, 4, 5, 6, 7, and 8 in the seven succeeding ones.

Upon the conclusion of the last round, all release points, place their swords over right shoulders, face counter-clockwise round the ring (turning clockwise), grasp the points of the swords in front of them, and dance round to the end of the strain.

Figure 7.-- Right-Shoulder Lock.

Passing right arms over their heads, all face centre, separate hands and, still moving round, make the Lock, each passing his right hand under the left hand of the dancer on his right, and his left hand over the right hand of the dancer on his left (8 bars, B music).

Figure 8.—The Wheel.

All walk round clockwise, while the leader raises the Lock high above his head, holding it in his right hand, arm erect, by the hilt of his own sword. During the first bar of the music, he inclines the Lock backward and passes it to No. 2, who grasps it in his right hand by the hilt of his own sword. In the second bar, No. 2 passes the Lock to No. 3 in like manner. This movement is continued, each dancer in turn grasping the Lock by his own hilt, and passing it to the dancer behind him ; so that by the end of the strain the Lock is once again in the possession of the leader (8 bars, A music).

FIGURE 9.—THE ROSE.

The Clown now enters the ring, the Lock is placed round his neck, while the dancers walk round, clockwise, each holding the hilt of his own sword. On the middle beat of the last bar all draw their swords from the Lock and place them over their right shoulders; whereupon, the Clown falls down, as though dead (8 bars, B music).

The Besom-Betty then runs into the ring, kneels down beside the Clown, tends him, and finally revives him. She then helps him on to his feet and, giving him her arm, walks out of the ring with him.

This brings the dance to a conclusion.

NOTATION.

Fig. 1. The Clash (*see* p. 28).
Fig. 2. The Snake (*see* p. 39).
Fig. 3. Single-over (*see* p. 88).
Fig. 4. Single-under (*see* p. 88).
Fig. 5. Double-over (*see* p. 89).
Fig. 6. Double-under (*see* p. 89).
Fig. 7. Right-shoulder Lock (*see* p. 89).
Fig. 8. The Wheel (*see* p. 89).
Fig. 9. The Rose (*see* p. 90).

CHAPTER II.

THE SHORT-SWORD DANCE.

THE WINLATON SWORD DANCE.

WINLATON is a small mining village on the Durham side of the Tyne, close to Newcastle. A sword dance has been danced there every Christmas within living memory, though of late years the performances have become rather irregular.

The dance is, perhaps, the most primitive example of its kind now to be seen in the North of England. It would be difficult to exaggerate the force and energy with which it was executed when I saw it in December, 1912. The performers were men well-advanced in years—the leader, Mr. William Prudhoe, is sixty-five years old—and, although the dance is a short one, they were quite exhausted by their efforts.

Although its figures are few in number, and none of them, technically, of special intricacy—compared, at least, with those of the Earsdon and other dances—the dance is by no means an easy one. The great difficulty is to catch its barbaric spirit, to reproduce the breathless speed, the sureness and economy of movement, the vigour and abandonment of the "stepping," displayed by the Winlaton men. The movements must be absolutely continuous, and, from the conclusion of the Calling-on Song to the final exhibition of the Nut, there must be no stop or pause of any kind.

There are five dancers, a Betty, and a musician who plays a tin-whistle.

COSTUME.

The dancers wear white shirts, sparsely decorated back and front with ribbons, dark trousers and belt, and have nothing on their heads. Each man carries a rapper of the usual type, but of smaller dimensions than those used by the Earsdon and Swalwell men. The blade from hilt to tip is nineteen inches in length by one-and-an-eighth in width, and the revolving handle is three inches long, making twenty-two inches over all.

The Betty, a man-woman, wears a bonnet and a dress of coloured stuff, and carries a rapper. Holding her sword horizontally above her head, harlequin-fashion, she dances up and down outside the dancers, throughout the performance, encouraging them from time to time with wild and uncouth cries.

THE MUSIC.

The tune to which the Calling-on Song is sung is a dorian variant of the Irish air, " Colleen dhas," the tune which is usually sung by English folk-singers to " The green, mossy banks of the Lea " (*see* " Folk-Songs from Somerset," No. 67).

The jig tune, played between the stanzas of the song, is the first strain of " The Tenpenny Bit." No special air is associated with the dance itself, various jig tunes being played by the musician at his discretion. In the accompanying music-book (*see* " The Sword Dances of Northern England : Songs and Dance Airs," Set III.), " The Tenpenny Bit " and " Irish Whisky " are given ; and these, it is suggested, should be played to alternate figures.

As already stated, there is no pause between the figures. The musician, however, should always play the second strain (B) of the music to the Ring, the movement which concludes each section of the dance, and then change the tune for the succeeding figure. The exhibition of the Nut, at the conclusion of the dance, should be accompanied with the second strain of the music (B).

THE STEP.

Except where otherwise directed in the instructions the dancers perform the movements at a rapid, elastic, walking step, executed on the ball of the foot, at the rate of 160 steps to the minute. When directed to "step," they are to dance in the way explained in the Grenoside dance (*see* Part I., p. 56), as vigorously and rhythmically as they can.

THE DANCE.

The dancers stand in a ring, facing centre, each holding his rapper erect in front of him in his right hand, hilt at breast-level, thus:—

Bottom.

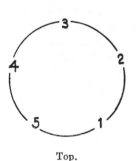

Top.

Audience.

The Betty then walks round in a small circle, clockwise, between the dancers and the audience, and sings the following song, the dancers singing in unison with her the last line of each verse.

CALLING·ON SONG.

(1)   Good people, give ear to my story;
      I've called here to see you by chance,
      And I've brought you five lads blithe and bonny,
      Intending to give you a dance.
      Winlaton is our habitation,
      The place we were all born and bred,
      There's not finer boys in the nation,
      And none are so gallantly led.

(2)   The first is the son of bold Elliot,
      The first youth to enter the ring,
      And, I'm proud and rejoicing to tell it,
      He fought for his country and King.
      He would conquer or else he would die;
      Bold Elliot defended the place;
      Their plans he soon caused them to alter,
      Some fled and some fell in disgrace.

(3)   Now my next handsome youth for to enter,
      He's a lad we've got very few such;
      His father beat the great Duke of Wintle,
      And fought with the fleet of the Dutch.
      His father he was the Lord Duncan,
      Who played the Dutch ne'er such a prank
      That they from their harbours went shrieking,
      And fled to the Doggety Bank.

(4)   The next is as bold a descendant,
      Lord Nelson, who fought on the Nile;
      Few men had more courage or talent;
      The Frenchmen he did them beguile.
      When the Frenchmen they nearly decoyed him,
      The battle he managed so well,
      In the fortress he completely destroyed them;
      Scarce one did get home for to tell.

(5)　Now my next handsome youth for to enter,
　　　He 's a lad of abilities bright :
　　　Ten thousand bright guineas I'll venture
　　　That he like his father would fight.
　　　At Waterloo and Talaveras
　　　Lord Wellington made the French fly.
　　　You scarcely could find such another,
　　　He'd conquer or else he would die.

(6)　Now my last handsome youth for to enter,
　　　He 's a lad that is straight and is tall ;
　　　He 's a son to yon big Buonaparty,
　　　The hero who conquered them all.
　　　He went over the Lowlands like thunder ;
　　　Made nations to quiver and shake ;
　　　Many thousands stood gazing with wonder
　　　At the havocs he always did make.

(7)　O now you see my five actors,
　　　The only five actors so bold,
　　　And they bear as good a charàcter
　　　As ever did stand upon earth.
　　　And if they're as good as their sires,
　　　Their deeds are deserving record ;
　　　So, lads, all the company desires
　　　To see how you handle your swords.

At the conclusion of each stanza, the musician plays the
first strain of " The Tenpenny Bit " (8 bars, A music), to
which the dancers, standing as above directed, " step " very
vigorously.

During the singing of the second stanza, No. 1 leaves the
ring and walks round in front of the Betty, returning to his
place at the conclusion of the verse for the " stepping." In
the four following stanzas, Nos. 2, 3, 4 and 5, in turn, leave
the ring and walk round in front of the Betty, each
returning to his place at the end of the verse.

After the "stepping" at the conclusion of the final verse of the song, the Betty moves away, the musician strikes up the dance air and the dancers perform the following figures.

Figure 1.—Ring-Clash-and-Step.

All dance round, clockwise, each placing his left arm over the left shoulder of the man in front, while holding his rapper erect, hilt at breast-level, and extending his right hand toward the centre of the circle (8 bars, A music). The pace should be so regulated that at the conclusion of this movement Nos. 1 and 5 may be at the top with their backs to the audience, thus :—

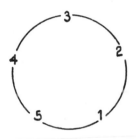

Audience.

On the first beat of the first bar of the following strain, all clash their swords together, place them over their left shoulders, each grasping with his left hand the tip of the sword in front of him, and, standing still, "step" (8 bars, B music).

Figure 2.—The Nut, Rose, and Ring.

(a) The Nut.

Nos. 1 and 5 stand still and make an arch with the sword between them (No. 5's). No. 1 makes rather more than a whole turn counter-clockwise; while, simultaneously, Nos. 2, 3, and 4 move forward together under the arch, face centre by turning counter-clockwise, separate their hands and lock the swords together, hilts under points. This operation must be executed very smartly, and should be completed in two bars of the music or even less.

(b) THE ROSE.

Immediately the Nut is tied the dancers raise it above their heads, horizontally, and "step" to the end of the phrase (8 bars, A music).

(c) THE RING.

The Nut is now lowered to waist-level and all move rapidly round in a ring, clockwise (8 bars, B music) to the following step, which is executed sideways, the legs alternately opening and closing scissor-fashion :—

so regulating their pace that at the conclusion of the movement Nos. 1 and 5 are facing the audience, thus :—

Bottom.

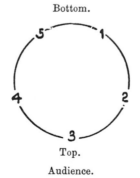

Top.

Audience.

The above movement is an extraordinarily effective one, when properly executed. The dancers should incline outward a little, keep their feet fairly close together, take short steps, and move, or whirl, round rapidly and rhythmically.

FIGURE 3. — THE NEEDLE.

The dancers bring their hands together and loosen the swords. Whereupon, No. 1 moves forward (*i.e.*, up) and, followed by Nos. 2 and 3, turns to his left and moves round in a small circle counter-clockwise. Simultaneously, No. 5 moves forward and, followed by No. 4 (who turns out to his right, clockwise), moves round in a small circle, clockwise. This initiates the Needle, which, from this point, is danced in precisely the same way as in the Swalwell dance (*see* Part I., p. 77), No. 3 changing from one circle to the other in alternate circuits.

This movement is continued until No. 1 calls " Nut," when the dancers at once repeat Figure 2. No. 1 must be careful to make the call when he and No. 5 are at the top, facing the audience, and when No. 3 is in his circle, thus :—

Bottom.

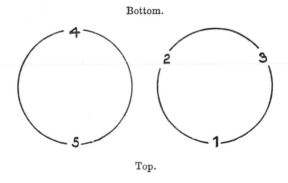

Top.

Audience.

FIGURE 4.—THE FIDDLER.

Nos. 1 and 5, who are now facing the audience, raise the sword between them (No. 5's). No. 1 then makes a whole turn clockwise, while, simultaneously, Nos. 2, 3 and 4 move down together, pass under the arch, turn clockwise, face up (2 bars), and stand thus :—

Bottom.

4   2

3

5   1

Top.

Audience.

No. 3, standing in the centre, holds his hands at breast-level with No. 2's sword over his left shoulder and his own sword over his right shoulder; while No. 1 rests his own sword, and No. 5 that of No. 4, on inside shoulders. Standing thus all "step" to the end of the phrase (8 bars).

No. 5 now lowers his sword, over which No. 3 leaps, and all "step" (8 bars).

No. 5 again lowering his sword, No. 3 leaps over it backward, returning to his place, and all "step" (8 bars).

Whereupon the dancers repeat Figure 2.

Figure 5.—Mary Anne.

The beginning of this Figure is executed in the same way as that of the preceding Figure, the dancers falling into the formation shown in the diagram.

No. 1, raising his left arm, then turns out to his left and, followed by No. 2, dances completely round No. 3, counter-clockwise, and returns to his place; while, simultaneously

No. 5, raising his right arm, turns out to his right and, followed by No. 4, dances completely round No. 3, clockwise, and returns to his place. When the two couples meet, behind and in front of No. 3, Nos. 1 and 2 pass *inside* Nos. 5 and 4.

Upon reaching his place, No. 1, followed by No. 2, makes a complete turn (or loop) counter-clockwise, and again dances round No. 3, counter-clockwise; while, upon reaching his place, No. 5, followed by No. 4, makes a complete turn (or loop) clockwise, and again dances round No. 3, clockwise. When the two couples meet in the second circuit, Nos. 1 and 2 pass *outside* Nos. 5 and 4.

Upon the completion of the second circuit, Nos. 1 and 5, followed respectively by Nos. 2 and 4, make a complete turn (or loop) as before, No. 1 counter-clockwise, No. 5 clockwise, and face the audience. Whereupon, without pause, Figure 2 is repeated.

Figure 6.—The Roll.

All, except No. 5 (who stands in his place throughout the figure), face counter-clockwise and raise their hands. No. 1, followed by Nos. 2, 3, and 4, then moves down in front of No. 5 (*i.e.*, between No. 5 and the centre of the circle), turns to his left and moves round in a circle, counter-clockwise, twice. At the beginning of each circuit, No. 5, as No. 1 passes him, raises both hands and makes a whole turn clockwise.

On the completion of the second circuit, No. 5 moves forward to his place in the ring, all face centre, separate hands, lock the swords together and then dance the Rose and the Ring of Figure 2.

Figure 7.—Straight Line.

No. 1 makes a whole turn, clockwise, and faces the audience; while Nos. 2, 3, and 4 move forward under No. 5's sword and stand in line facing the audience; No. 2 turning to his right, making a whole turn clockwise and standing on No. 1's left; No. 4 turning to his left and standing on No. 5's right; No. 3 making a half-turn, clockwise, and standing between Nos. 5 and 1 (2 bars), thus :—

4   5   3   1   2

It will be found that, when the hands are lowered to hip-level, Nos. 4 and 1 have their hands crossed right over left, and Nos. 5 and 2 have theirs crossed left over right; while No. 3 has his hands wide apart.

Standing in this position all "step" to the end of the strain (8 bars).

No. 3 now moves forward and makes a half-turn counter-clockwise; No. 2 turns out to his left, makes a whole turn counter-clockwise, passes behind No. 1, and stands between Nos. 1 and 3; while No. 4 turns out to his right, passes behind No. 5 and moves up between Nos. 5 and 3. Simultaneously, No. 1 makes a whole turn counter-clockwise (2 bars). This ties the Nut. Whereupon the remaining movements of Figure 2, the Rose and the Ring, are again repeated.

At the conclusion of the Ring, No. 1 raises the Nut in his right hand, arm erect, and all stand in line, facing the audience, thus,

4   5   1   2   3

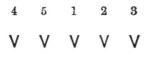

Audience.

and "step" to the end of the tune (8 bars, B music).

This brings the dance to a conclusion.

NOTATION.

THE NORTH WALBOTTLE SWORD DANCE.

WALBOTTLE is a suburb of Newcastle-on-Tyne. The sword dance, which is now annually performed at Christmas-time, was introduced there as recently as 1906 by a dancer of the name of Raine, who taught the Walbottle men the sword dance which used to be, but is not now, danced at his native village, Bedlington. The dance now to be described is, therefore, strictly speaking, the Bedlington dance.

There are five dancers, a Tommy or Fool, a Bessy, and a concertina-player.

COSTUME.

The dancers are dressed in white cambric shirts with a sailor-knotted tie of velvet, violet velveteen breeches, white stockings of rough texture, black shoes, and a broad sash of yellow silk or sateen round the waist, tied in a bow over the left hip. Each dancer carries a rapper of the ordinary pattern, but of thicker metal than usual. The blade is twenty-four inches long by one-and-an-eighth wide, and the revolving handle five inches in length, making twenty-nine inches in all.

The Bessy, a man-woman, has a bonnet and chignon, and a dress of crimson-flowered calico with a ribbon round the waist.

The Tommy wears a tall hat, a tail-coat, and loose trousers of the same material as the Bessy's dress, and a false moustache and beard. Both he and the Bessy carry swords.

THE MUSIC.

There is no special tune belonging to the dance. The airs usually played are "Irish Whisky," "The Rollicking Irishman," and "The Irish Washerwoman."

The figures of the dance are performed without break. The music controls the steps only, except in those movements for which a definite number of bars is prescribed in the following instructions.

The musician should always accompany the Rose with the second strain (B) of the tune, at any rate when he intends to change the air in the next Nut.

THE STEP.

In the ordinary figures, the dancers use a springy, short-paced walking step, executed on the ball of the foot, at the rate of 140 to 160 per minute. In the Rose, and where otherwise directed, they "step" in the way described in the Grenoside dance (*see* Part I., p. 56).

THE DANCE.

Clash-and-Turn-Single.

The performers, swords over right shoulders, stand in a large circle, twelve or fifteen feet in diameter, facing centre thus :

Bottom.

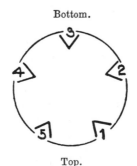

Top.

Audience.

and remain in this position while the musician plays the first strain of the air (8 bars).

At the beginning of the next strain all take three running-steps forward on the first and middle beats of the first bar and the first beat of the second bar, and clash their swords together on the middle beat of the second bar. In the third and fourth bars each dancer makes a whole turn on his axis, counter-clockwise, in four steps, beginning with the right foot. At the beginning of the fifth bar all face clockwise, turning clockwise to do so, place rappers over right (*i.e.*, inside) shoulders, grasp with left hands the tips of the swords in front and at once break into Single-guard, the first movement of the first Nut.

In construction, the Walbottle dance is similar to the Swalwell and Earsdon dances. It consists, that is, of a series of Figures or Nuts, each containing three movements— (1) Single-guard, (2) a distinctive movement varying with each Figure and ending with the tying of the Nut, and (3) the Rose.

Single-Guard.

Single-guard is the same as One-turn-off of the Swalwell dance (*see* Part I., p. 74).

The Nut and Rose.
(*a*) The Nut.

The normal way of tying the Nut at Walbottle is a compromise between the two methods used, respectively, at Swalwell and Winlaton.

Bottom.

Top.
Audience.

No. 1 makes a three-quarter turn, counter-clockwise, and faces No. 5, who raises his sword and makes an arch. Simultaneously, Nos. 1 and 5 move down a step or two and pass the raised sword over the heads of Nos. 4, 3 and 2, who together move up under the arch, face centre by turning counter-clockwise, separate hands and lock the swords together, hilts under points. This operation should be executed very smartly, in two bars of the music if possible. The leader should call " Nut," a bar or two before the end of a strain, so that the Rose may be begun at the commencement of the next strain, which, as already stated, should always be the concluding one (B) of the tune.

When the Nut is tied in the way above described, the leader should always, if possible, give the call when he and No. 5 are at the top, *i.e.*, nearest the audience. Then, when the Nut is tied, Nos. 1 and 5 will be at the lower end, facing the audience.

The Nut is, of course, untied by a reverse movement, No. 1 turning clockwise, Nos. 2, 3 and 4 moving down under the sword, and all (except No. 5) turning clockwise to face centre. This is the method by which, in the absence of instructions to the contrary, the Nut is always to be tied.

(*b*) THE ROSE.

The Rose is usually danced in the same way as at Earsdon, all standing in a ring and " stepping " while the Nut is raised to a horizontal position (*see* Part I., p. 90). Sometimes, however, after holding up the Nut horizontally for a couple of bars, the dancers leave the Nut in the hands of No. 1 and fall back into line facing the audience, returning to the original Rose position at the end of the strain. This variation, however, is scarcely to be recommended. It seems better to dance the Rose in the normal way, and to reserve the formal exhibition of the Nut, in line, for the conclusion of the dance.

It should be noted that in two cases, Number-one-ring and Number-three-ring, the Rose is danced in a different way, as will be seen in the directions.

The distinctive movements of the several Figures will now be described. It may be said, in passing, that the order in which these are performed is determined by the leader, who usually calls out the name of the next movement during the performance of Single-guard. The order in which the movements are here presented is that which the Walbottle men observed when they were good enough to dance to me.

CURLY.

No. 1, raising both hands, turns out to his left and, followed by Nos. 2 and 3, moves round in a small circle counter-clockwise; while, simultaneously, No. 5, raising both hands, turns out to his right and, followed by No. 4, moves round in a small circle clockwise.

This movement is, of course, the same as Figure 2 of the Beadnell dance (*see* Part II., p. 41), and similar to Three-and-two of the Swalwell dance (*see* Part I., p. 77), except that No. 3, instead of changing from one circle to the other in alternate circuits, remains throughout in No. 1's circle.

The leader should call " Nut " when he and No. 5 have just completed a circuit and are facing the audience, and, if possible, when near the end of one or other of the strains of the music.

FIGURE-OF-EIGHT.

This is danced in very much the same way as Right and left in the Swalwell dance (*see* Part I., p. 79), the dancers, however, following one another in a different order.

The movement begins in the same way as Curly; Nos. 2 and 3 following No. 1 in the right-hand circle, No. 4 following No. 5 in the left-hand circle. The two sets of dancers change their respective circles at the end of each circuit, crossing from one circle to the other in the following order: Nos. 1, 5, 2, 4, and 3.

The leader must, of course, call "Nut" when he has just completed a circuit in his own circle, *i.e.*, the right-hand one.

Number-One-Ring.

All move round in a ring, hilt-and-point, hands at hip-level, clockwise, for one complete circuit. They then raise both hands, make a half-turn counter-clockwise, stand close together back to back, and lock the swords together above their heads, each man placing his left hand under the right hand of his right neighbour, and his right hand over the left hand of his left neighbour.

The Rose is now danced in the following way. The leader raises the Nut vertically in his right hand, while all "step," standing back to back (8 bars). He then lowers it to its original position and all grasp their swords as before, make a half-turn clockwise, and face centre. This, of course, unties the Nut.

Fast-Nut.

This begins in the same way as Curly (*see* p. 107). After the dancers have made two or more circuits, at a signal from the leader all cross over from one circle to the other, as in Figure-of-eight (*see* p. 107). They now move round in their wrong circles, *i.e.*, Nos. 1, 2, and 3 clockwise in the left circle, Nos. 5 and 4 counter-clockwise in the right circle, and continue to do so until, at a signal from the leader, they return to their own circles, crossing in the same order as before, viz., Nos. 1, 5. 2, 4, and 3. The Nut is then immediately tied.

FOUR-CORNER.

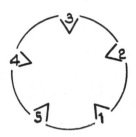

Nos. 5 and 1 make each a half-turn, clockwise and counter-clockwise respectively, and face audience. Simultaneously, No. 2 moves forward under No. 5's sword, backs under No. 1's sword and stands on No. 1's left, facing audience; No. 4 moves forward under No. 5's sword, backs under his own sword and stands on No. 5's right, facing the audience; while No. 3 moves forward and stands between Nos. 1 and 5, thus :—

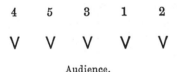

Audience.

All "step" in this formation to the end of the strain (8 bars). Nos. 2 and 3 now lower their swords, over which Nos. 1 and 5, respectively, jump, and all "step" to the end of the strain (8 bars).

No. 3 then makes a half-turn, counter-clockwise, places his back against No. 5's sword, turns a back-somersault over it, and all "step" (8 bars).

Nos. 1 and 5 now move backward a step (No. 1 under No. 2's sword, No. 5 under No. 3's), and all face centre, Nos. 1 and 4 each making a whole turn counter-clockwise. This ties the Nut.

Number-two Ring.

All move round, clockwise, hilt-and-point, until Nos. 1 and 5 are at the bottom, thus :—

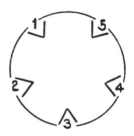

Raising their hands, all make a half-turn counter clockwise, stand close together, back to back, and "step" (8 bars).

No. 1 then lowers his sword and stands still; while No. 2, right hand up, jumps over it, turns to his left, and still holding the sword down, moves round counter-clockwise to No. 1, Nos. 3, 4, and 5 successively jumping over the sword and turning to their left. No. 1 then turns counter-clockwise, faces centre, and the Nut is tied.

Navvy.

This begins in the same way as Curly (*see* p. 107).

At the end of the first circuit Nos. 2 and 3 cross over into the left circle, and No. 4 into the right (leaving Nos. 1 and 5 each in his own circle), the three dancers crossing, at the junction of the loops, in the following order : Nos. 2, 4, and 3. At the end of the next circuit Nos. 2, 3, and 4 cross back again to their own circles. This dual movement is continued as long as the leader elects, the Nut being called only when all are in their proper circles.

CRAMPER.

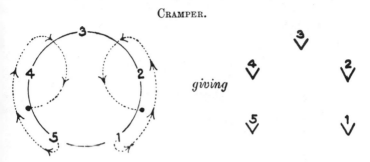

No. 5, raising his right arm, turns out to his right, passes between Nos. 4 and 3, and stands in front of No. 4, facing the audience; while, simultaneously, No. 1, raising his left arm, turns out to his left, passes between Nos. 2 and 3, and stands in front of No. 2, facing the audience.

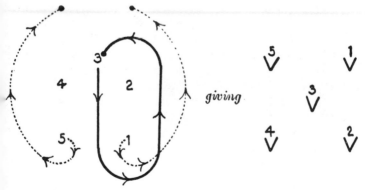

No. 3 now moves forward between Nos. 5 and 1, turns to his left and passes completely round No. 2, No. 1 following him part of the way only, coming to a halt behind No. 2, facing audience. Simultaneously, No. 5, turning out to his right, moves behind No. 4 and stays there facing audience. During these operations Nos. 2 and 4 stand still, No. 4 turning round on his axis once, clockwise, and No. 2 twice, counter-clockwise.

No. 3 again moves forward between Nos. 2 and 4, turns counter-clockwise and faces centre.   No. 5 makes a whole turn counter-clockwise, and all face centre.   This ties the Nut.

NUMBER-THREE-RING.

Down.

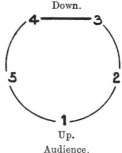

Up.

Audience.

Nos. 3 and 4 hold up the sword between them (No. 3's), face each other, and make an arch.   Nos. 5, 1, and 2, in order, then pass under the arch, turn to their right, and return to their places.   All now face outward, Nos. 5, 1, and 2 making a quarter-turn counter-clockwise, No. 3 a quarter-turn clockwise, and No. 4 rather more than a whole turn counter-clockwise.   All, standing close together, back to back, now lock the swords together above their heads, by separating their hands and bending points under hilts.

The Rose is then performed in the following way.   The leader holds up the Nut in his right hand, arm erect, and all, still standing back to back, " step " to the end of the strain.

The leader now lowers the Nut to its original horizontal position, all grasp their own swords as before, and the Nut is untied in the following way : Nos. 2, 1, and 5 turn clockwise, move round outside No. 3, turn to their left and pass *up* under No. 3's sword and return to places, turning to their left. Directly No. 5 has passed through the arch, No. 4 makes rather more than a whole turn, clockwise, No. 3 makes a half-turn counter-clockwise and all face centre.

STAND-IN-THE-GUARD.

All face the audience, hilt-and-point, and stand thus :—

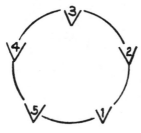

Audience.

No. 3, moving forward, jumps over No. 5's sword, and all
" step " (8 bars).

No. 3 now turns a back-somersault over No. 5's sword, and
all " step " (8 bars).

The Nut is then tied in the usual way.

Directly the Nut is untied, and when all are in hilt-and-
point formation, the Tommy joins the dancers and comes into
the ring between Nos. 2 and 3. After two or three circuits,
clockwise, have been danced, three of the Nuts are repeated,
as follows :—

CURLY (for 6).

As before (*see* p. 107), Tommy and No. 2 following No. 1,
Nos. 4 and 3 following No. 5.

FIGURE-OF-EIGHT (for 6).

As before (*see* p. 107), the dancers in the first circuit
following one another as in the preceding Figure, and then
crossing in this order : 1, 5, 2, 3, Tommy, 4.

Four-Corner (for 6).

As before (*see* p. 109), the dancers lining up thus :—

4	5	3	1	Tommy	2
V	V	V	V	V	V

Audience.

At the conclusion of the last Nut, the Bessy joins the dance, coming into the ring between Nos. 4 and 3. After two or three circuits clockwise, hilt-and-point, have been danced, three of the Figures, above described, are repeated, as follows :—

Curly (for 7).

As before (*see* p. 107), No. 2, Tommy and No. 3 following No. 1 ; No. 4 and Bessy following No. 5.

Stand-in-the-Guard (for 7).

As before (*see* p. 113), the dancers standing in the following formation :

```
              3
              V
   Bessy          Tommy
     V              V
     4              2
     V              V
     5              1
     V              V
          Audience.
```

Four-Corner (for 7).

As before (*see* p. 109), the dancers standing thus :

4	Bessy	5	3	1	Tommy	2
V	V	V	V	V	V	V

Audience.

Directly the Rose in the last Nut is concluded, the leader raises the Nut in his right hand, arm erect, while the rest of the dancers line up, three on each side, face audience and "step" to the end of the strain (8 bars, B music).

This brings the dance to a conclusion.

NOTATION.

Clash-and-Turn-single (*see* p. 104).

> *Each of the following movements is preceded by Single-guard (see p. 105), and followed by the tying of the Nut (see p. 105) and the Rose (see p. 106).*

Curly (*see* p. 107).
Figure-of eight (*see* p. 107).
Number-one-ring (*see* p. 108).
Fast-nut (*see* p. 108).
Four-corner (*see* p. 109).
Number-two-ring (*see* p. 110).
Navvy (*see* p. 110).
Cramper (*see* p. 111).
Number-three-ring (*see* p. 112).
Stand-in-the-guard (*see* p. 113).
Curly (for 6) (*see* p. 113).
Figure-of-eight (for 6) (*see* p. 113).
Four-corner (for 6) (*see* p. 114).
Curly (for 7) (*see* p. 114).
Stand-in-the-guard (for 7) (*see* p. 114).
Four-corner (for 7) (*see* p. 114).
Exhibition of the Nut in line (*see* p. 115).

———

N.B.—*Dancers, other than skilled gymnasts, are advised to substitute a backward jump for the back somersault which occurs several times in this dance, and is a dangerous movement.*